ω
2.50

D0735545

THE PASSOVER HAGGADAH

הגדה של פסח

THE PASSOVER HAGGADAH

With a Traditional and Contemporary Commentary by
Rabbi SHLOMO RISKIN

הגדה של פסח

KTAV PUBLISHING HOUSE, INC.
NEW YORK

COPYRIGHT © 1983
BY SHLOMO RISKIN

ISBN: 0-88125-014-7

MANUFACTURED IN THE UNITED STATES OF AMERICA

This Haggadah is dedicated to
חיה בילא בת שלמה הכהן
my beloved grandmother ע״ה, who first taught me to
appreciate the richness of the Passover Seder, and to
אביבה פרידא לאה בת דוד בער שתחי׳
my beloved life-partner, who has enabled me to
celebrate the beauty of the Passover Seder with our
family and extended family each year.

Preface

This work is not a typical Haggadah. Its purpose is not to offer a new translation or provide running commentary for the Hebrew text. Nor does it dwell upon the historic and halachic aspects of the Seder ritual. Instead, I have attempted to use the Haggadah as a source for discussing and elaborating upon a score of themes that are basic to Judaism. In this work the Haggadah becomes a gateway to a deeper understanding of Jewish thought and ritual. Such fundamental concepts as freedom, messianism, particularism vs. universalism, and others are shown to be intrinsic to the Haggadah.

At the same time I have not ignored the particular historic and religious character of Passover and how that is reflected in the Seder service. From the chanting of Kiddush to the recitation of Hallel at the end of the Seder, I have tried to link the ritual with the conceptual— to show how our prayers and recitations reflect the essence of Passover.

This Haggadah is not an "ordinary" one in another sense. It did not start out in my library or study hall with pencil and paper in hand. It began with my *Shabbat ha-Gadol* discourses, which were later expanded into a series of taped talks on the Haggadah. Some of the material came from the model Seders that I conducted over the past few years in my synagogue. Finally my own family Seder has been a valuable stimulant for some of the concepts and thoughts that you will find recorded herein.

The oral rather than literary genesis of this Haggadah allows for a more personal touch. Arranged in the form of a series of homilies, each one appropriate to the text to which it is appended, the Haggadah speaks directly to the reader. It is as if you are sitting at my very own Seder. Come, let us begin!

Introduction

To be a Jew means to live in a universe of stucture and purpose. To be a Jew means to feel part of a historic process guided by a God of love and concern and leading towards a world of peace and fulfillment. To be a Jew means to be a unique link in the great chain of Jewish being, to be crowned with the glory of majestic faith in freedom for all humanity, to be charged with the mission of imparting compassion and morality to an often insensitive and apathetic world. To be a Jew means to belong to a very special family within the family of nations, to relive that family's joys and tragedies, and to build one's future upon the experiences of the past. To be a Jew means to be together even in a society where so many are alone, to derive security from deep roots even in a society where so many are struggling merely to remain afloat, to be inspired with significance even in a society where so many are bored and cynical. This description of the Jew is remarkably expressed throughout that mystical and magical evening known as the Passover Seder.

Acknowledgments

One of the most important lessons that the Haggadah teaches us is *hakorat hatov*—the obligation to express gratitude to those who have helped us. In the course of bringing this Haggadah to light, I have been assisted by many friends and colleagues. Due to my heavy communal and synagogal obligations, I have needed all the more their advice and encouragement.

There are several people who merit special mention. First and foremost, I wish to thank Rabbi Joseph B. Soloveitchik, my revered teacher and mentor, whose fertility of thought and creativity of mind have left an indelible mark on Jewish law and philosophy. Many of the ideas expressed herein came directly or indirectly from the *shiurim, yahrzeit* discourses, and other public lectures that the Rav has given in the course of his lifetime, may God grant him many more years.

Before a work can be published, it needs a powerful moving force. In this case, it was Rabbi Nochum Stillerman. As executive director of Ohr Torah Institute, and a faithful friend and confidant, he urged me and encouraged me to make my ideas on the Haggadah more widely known than the confines of my school and synagogue would allow. The taping of my lectures and later the transcribing of the tapes were due to his efforts.

I am deeply grateful to my devoted congregant Ernest Weiss, who was responsible for the technical details in the taping and transcribing process. With unstinting diligence and devotion, he converted the oral into the written. It is because of him that my spoken word does not remain transient.

Credit for extensively revising this work, while it was still in manuscript form, goes to my dedicated colleague and friend Rabbi Isaac Mann, who on occasion injected his own insightful ideas into the text. He was responsible for taking what was basically a series of oral discourses and transforming them into a carefully constructed literary work.

I also wish to thank Bernard Scharfstein and Irving Ruderman of Ktav Publishing House who diligently saw this volume through the press.

אחרון אחרון חביב. None of my accomplishments, and certainly

not this Haggadah, would have been possible without the constant support and encouragement of my beloved wife, Vicky. Not only has she established the home atmosphere which has been conducive to my work, but also many of my interpretations have their origin in her most original and creative insights. שלי ושלכם שלה.

And finally I am most grateful to the Almighty for giving me the will, opportunity, and health to labor in His vineyard.

The Origin of the Word "Haggadah"

The Haggadah is one of the most popular Hebrew works. Going back—at least in skeletal form—to the time of the Mishnah, it has long been a favorite source of study and inspiration. Commentators and homilists have pored over its words while artists and illustrators have labored to adorn its pages. No other work has captured the love and enthusiasm of the Jewish people as has the Haggadah.

The name of the work comes from *le-haggid,* "to tell," which refers to the biblical commandment of וְהִגַּדְתָּ לְבִנְךָ—"And you shall tell your child on that day that because of this [viz., the observance of the mitzvot] God did these things for me when I came out of Egypt" (Ex. 13:8).

The use of the verb "to tell" (לְהַגִּיד) by the Torah rather than the more common "to say" (לֵאמֹר) implies that the Exodus has to be recounted as if one were "telling" or informing someone, not just reciting. The language and style are to be geared to the level and disposition of the listeners, for the all-important concern is that the narrated events and their meaning be understood. Thus, the Haggadah refers later to Four Sons, each of whom is *told* in a different manner.

In our time, when many do not understand even the simple Hebrew of the Haggadah, it may be recited in English, at least in part. However, the blessings and the most significant passages should be repeated in Hebrew.

To "Tell" and to "Remember"

Besides the mitzvah of "to tell," the Torah also instructs us "to remember" (the day of the Exodus). Let us examine carefully three verses, each of which refers to one or the other obligation.°

° See also Ex. 13:14—. . . וְהָיָה כִּי יִשְׁאָלְךָ בִנְךָ מָחָר.

. . . וְהִגַּדְתָּ לְבִנְךָ בַּיּוֹם הַהוּא—And you shall tell your child on that day . . . (Ex. 13:8).

. . . זָכוֹר אֶת הַיּוֹם הַזֶּה—Remember this day [every year] on which you went free from Egypt, the house of bondage; how the Lord freed you with a mighty hand. You shall not eat any leavened bread (Ex. 13:3).

. . . לְמַעַן תִּזְכּוֹר—. . . so that you may remember the day of your going out of Egypt all the days of your life (Deut. 16:3).

How do these three verses relate to each other? We shall begin with a discussion of the last one and work our way backwards.

The Mishnah teaches: מַזְכִּירִים יְצִיאַת מִצְרַיִם בַּלֵּילוֹת—"we mention [even] at night the Exodus from Egypt" (*Berakhot* 1:4). On this basis Maimonides writes:

> Even though there is no commandment to wear the ritual fringes at night, we read [the third paragraph of the *Shema*] at night because it contains mention of the Exodus from Egypt. And there is a commandment to recall by day and by night the going out from Egypt, as it is written, "In order that you may remember the day of your going out from the land of Egypt all the days of your life" (Deut. 16:3) [and "*all* the days" includes the nights].
>
> (Laws of the *Shema* 1:3)

From the verse לְמַעַן תִּזְכּוֹר, Maimonides infers that we are commanded to remember the Exodus not only on the Seder night but on every night—and day—of the year. This mitzvah is fulfilled by a mental and verbal recollection of the ancient events, or what we might refer to as cognitive remembrance.

From the second verse we cited above, Maimonides derives the following:

> It is a positive commandment of the Torah to relate on the night of the fifteenth day of Nisan the miracles and the wonders which were done for our forefathers in Egypt, as it is written in the Torah, "Remember this day when you left Egypt," just as it is written, "Remember the Sabbath day to keep it holy."
>
> (Laws of Leavened and Unleavened Bread 7:1)

Maimonides' reference to the Sabbath is rather striking. What additional light does this association (viz., both commandments begin with "remember") shed on our mitzvah?

To resolve this question we must probe a little deeper into the concept of *zakhor* with respect to the Sabbath. We fulfill the mitzvah of *zakhor* through the act of *Kiddush,* in which we recall that God created the world in six days and rested on the seventh. But this verbal rite does not in and of itself encompass the whole notion of *zakhor.* What is also necessary is an "act" of imitation whereby we abstain from creative physical activity as God did on the primordial Sabbath. We remember through *imitatio dei. Zakhor* thus includes not only cognitive appreciation but also experiential imitation. We labor six days a week and rest on the Sabbath, making our week a replica—albeit in miniature—of the Divine week.

Similarly the *zakhor* of Pesach obligates us not only to relate verbally the events of the Exodus but also to relive experientially that momentous time. In contrast to the other days of the year, on the night of the fifteenth of Nisan passive, cognitive awareness is not enough; together with the *maggid* ("telling") there is the eating of the matzah, the swallowing of the *maror,* and the reciting of *Hallel.* We must eat the food that our fathers ate at the time of the Exodus, we must taste the bitterness that they felt at the time of their enslavement, and we must sing the psalms of joy that they sang at the moment of their deliverance. This is the meaning of the famous rabbinic dictum that we recite at the Seder: "And . . . because of *this* (בַּעֲבוּר זֶה), *this* referring to the matzah and *maror* that is placed on the Seder table." In sum, on the night of Pesach we do not merely commemorate the process of redemption but we relive it in its entirety. Thus we can appreciate Maimonides' association of the *zakhor* of the Sabbath with that of Pesach.

We have clarified the relationship of the verses לְמַעַן תִּזְכֹּר and זָכוֹר—the former a commandment to remember the Exodus mentally and verbally every day of the year, the latter a summons to reexperience the event on the fifteenth of Nisan. Now to the very first verse we cited above: וְהִגַּדְתָּ לְבִנְךָ—"and you shall tell your child."

The obligation to tell and retell the Exodus story to one's children lies at the heart of the Seder ritual. The very name *Haggadah,* literally "a retelling," is derived from וְהִגַּדְתָּ לְבִנְךָ, as we have mentioned. Apparently the intellectual and experiential is not sufficient; there must also be the didactic. The Exodus—the most crucial event in the Jewish historical consciousness—must not remain a self-reflective, contemplative experience thought out and even acted out on the Seder night by individuals qua individuals. It is a family, or communal, affair having as a central purpose the need to teach and inspire the next generation. Through our words and actions the children must feel a sense of participation. We can thereby become a link in the long continuity of Jewish existence.

The family quality of the Seder is rooted in biblical, rabbinic, and folk sources. In the Torah we are bidden to have the Pesach meal (when the sacrificial system was in effect) only in *havurot*— in predesignated groups. These groups consisted of families, including children, and guests. No other ritual meal was circumscribed in this manner. By the talmudic period many rituals had been incorporated into the Seder to ensure the participation of children, such as the Four Questions and the *karpas*. In later generations, the hiding of the *afikoman* and the chanting of children's songs were added to keep the children awake throughout the recitation of the Haggadah. Thus, we fulfill the mitzvah of וְהִגַּדְתָּ לְבִנְךָ by incorporating the didactic component into the very fabric of the Seder.

On a more homiletical plane, וְהִגַּדְתָּ can be understood as a means to transform the experiential—the *zakhor*—into the existential. As we relate the Exodus story to our children, we realize that the mere telling and even acting out of history are not enough. We need to become a link for them to the past. We must convey to the next generation the national identity of their forebears. We do this by becoming our ancestors spiritually—by sharing their pain, by rejoicing in their freedom, by dreaming their dreams, by becoming them in essence. As we merge with them, so do our children merge with us. On this night parents and offspring become united as living links in the Jewish tradition.

One may look upon the three verses we have spoken of in a slightly different perspective, as representing three different timeframes. The first commandment, לְמַעַן תִּזְכֹּר, focuses upon the past; it is an instruction to recall the events of our ancient history. The second verse, זָכוֹר, relates to the present. We remember by reliving in the present what happened in the past, as if we ourselves had participated in the events of yore. The third prescription, וְהִגַּדְתָּ לְבִנְךָ, looks to the future—to the next generation—and requires that we instill in them a sense of identification with the Jewish people and its history. Taken together, these three mitzvot encompass every temporal sphere, thus emphasizing the all-inclusive quality of the Seder and the importance that should be attached to it.

SEARCHING FOR LEAVEN

בְּדִיקַת חָמֵץ

On the evening following the thirteenth of Nisan (if the first day of Passover is on Sunday, on the evening following the twelfth of Nisan), after the evening service, the head of the household makes the final preparation for Passover by searching for leaven throughout the house. It is customary to place ten pieces of bread in various places, so that when the search is made, leaven is found. Otherwise, the benediction recited before the ceremony would be in vain.

Before the ceremony of searching for leaven begins, a candle is lit and the following prayer is recited:

Blessed art Thou, Eternal our God, Ruler of the universe, Who made us holy with His commandments, and commanded us to remove the leaven.

בָּרוּךְ אַתָּה יְיָ, אֱלֹהֵינוּ מֶלֶךְ הָעוֹלָם, אֲשֶׁר קִדְּשָׁנוּ בְּמִצְוֹתָיו, וְצִוָּנוּ עַל בִּעוּר־חָמֵץ:

The search for leaven is conducted. After the leaven has been gathered and wrapped securely, the following is said:

Any leaven that may still be in the house, which I have not seen or have not removed, shall be as if it does not exist, and as the dust of the earth.

כָּל־חֲמִירָא וַחֲמִיעָא, דְּאִכָּא בִרְשׁוּתִי, דְּלָא חֲמִתֵּהּ, וּדְלָא בִעַרְתֵּהּ, וּדְלָא יְדַעְנָא לֵהּ, לִבָּטֵל וְלֶהֱוֵי הֶפְקֵר, כְּעַפְרָא דְאַרְעָא:

On the fourteenth of Nisan (if the first day of Passover is on Sunday, on the thirteenth of Nisan), about ten o'clock in the morning, all the leaven that has remained in the house together with all collected during the search the previous night is burned. At the burning of the leaven the following is recited:

Any leaven that may still be in the house, which I have or have not seen, which I have or have not removed, shall be as if it does not exist, and as the dust of the earth.

כָּל־חֲמִירָא וַחֲמִיעָא, דְּאִכָּא בִרְשׁוּתִי, (דַּחֲזִתֵּהּ וּדְלָא חֲזִתֵּהּ,) דַּחֲמִתֵּהּ וּדְלָא חֲמִתֵּהּ, דְּבִעַרְתֵּהּ וּדְלָא בִעַרְתֵּהּ, לִבָּטֵל וְלֶהֱוֵי הֶפְקֵר, כְּעַפְרָא דְאַרְעָא:

MIXING OF FOODS

עֵרוּב תַּבְשִׁילִין

When the first day of Passover falls on a Thursday, in order that it may be permissible to cook on Friday for Saturday (one is permitted to cook on a holiday for that day alone), the head of the household must perform the ritual of "Eruv Tavshilin" on Wednesday afternoon before the festival. This consists of taking a piece of matzah and some other cooked food, such as fish or meat, putting them on a plate, raising it, and then reciting the following prayers:

Blessed art Thou, Eternal our God, Ruler of the universe, Who made us holy with His commandments, and commanded us concerning the *Eruv*.

בָּרוּךְ אַתָּה יְיָ אֱלֹהֵינוּ מֶלֶךְ הָעוֹלָם, אֲשֶׁר קִדְּשָׁנוּ בְּמִצְוֹתָיו וְצִוָּנוּ עַל מִצְוַת־עֵרוּב:

With this *Eruv* it shall be permissible for us to bake, cook, and to keep the food warm, to light the candles, and to prepare all necessary things on the festival for the Sabbath. This shall be permitted to us and to all Jews who live in this city.

בַּהֲדֵין עֵרוּבָא יְהֵא שָׁרֵא לָנָא לְמֵיפָא, וּלְבַשָּׁלָא, וּלְאַצְלָיָא, וּלְאַטְמָנָא, וּלְאַדְלָקָא שְׁרָגָא, וּלְתַקָּנָא, וּלְמֶעְבַּד כָּל־צָרְכָנָא, מִיּוֹמָא טָבָא לְשַׁבַּתָּא. לָנוּ, וּלְכָל־יִשְׂרָאֵל, הַדָּרִים בָּעִיר הַזֹּאת:

THE PREPARATION OF THE TABLE

Three plates are placed on the table; in one put three matzot; in another, a shank bone and a roasted egg, some horseradish ("bitter herbs") and celery or parsley, also a compound formed of nuts, fruits and wine (ḥaroset); in a third, vinegar or salt water.

זרוע   ביצה

מרור

חרוסת   כרפס

ORDER OF THE PASSOVER SEDER

Recite the *Kiddush*	.קַדֵּשׁ
Wash the hands	.וּרְחַץ
Eat a green vegetable	.כַּרְפַּס
Break the middle matzah	.יַחַץ
Recite the Passover story	.מַגִּיד
Wash the hands	.רָחְצָה
Eat the matzah	.מוֹצִיא מַצָּה
Eat the bitter herb	.מָרוֹר
Eat the bitter herb and matzah together	.כּוֹרֵךְ
Serve the festival meal	.שֻׁלְחָן עוֹרֵךְ
Eat the *afikoman*	.צָפוּן
Say the grace after meal	.בָּרֵךְ
Recite the *Hallel*	.הַלֵּל
Conclude the Seder	.נִרְצָה

Recitation of the Kiddush

KADESH

קַדֵּשׁ

Each of the four cups of wine accompanies a specific mitzvah of the Passover Seder. The first cup belongs to the *kadesh*, what we commonly call *Kiddush*, and it is with this cup that we begin the Seder. The second cup is associated with the *maggid*, during which we tell the story of the Exodus. The third cup is joined to the *birkat ha-mazon*. The fourth and final cup, at the end of *Hallel*, is raised over the songs of praise to God in gratitude for our redemption.

Our Sages link these four cups to the four expressions of redemption in Exodus 6:6–7: וְהוֹצֵאתִי, I will take you out from under the burdens of Egypt; וְהִצַּלְתִּי, I will save you from their work; וְגָאַלְתִּי, I will redeem you with a strong arm and great judgments; and וְלָקַחְתִּי, I will take you unto Me for a nation.

The first pair of redemptive acts—I will take you out and I will save you—refers to "freedom *from*" the physical burdens and sufferings of Egypt. The second pair—I will redeem you and I will take you unto Me—expresses "freedom *for*." There is a promise of yet another Divine redemptive act one verse later. "And I will bring you to the land which I swore to give to Abraham, Isaac, and Jacob . . ." However, since the Israelites after leaving Egypt did not enter the Promised Land until forty years later, and, therefore, this was not an immediate event following the redemption from Egypt, we drink only four cups of wine. We shall have occasion to dwell on a possible fifth cup in greater detail in our discussion of *Hallel*.

The psalmist speaks of the cup of wine as the symbol of redemption: כּוֹס יְשׁוּעוֹת אֶשָּׂא וּבְשֵׁם ה' אֶקְרָא ("I will lift up the cup of salvation and call upon God's Name—Ps. 116:13). Wine is a symbol of joy, as is written, "Wine gladdens the heart of man" (Ps. 104:15). Passover night is a night of consummate joy because we extol the love and mercy of Almighty God, who redeemed a people who hardly knew Him and who were, according to tradition, barely more worthy of redemption than the Egyptians. Indeed, according to the Targum, the root meaning of the word *Pesach* is "mercy," signifying that the essence of the holiday is a celebration of God's mercy towards the Israelites.

Wine, to be sure, also has a less-than-salutary aspect. Our Sages understood only too well the dangers inherent in this beverage. A charming midrash relates that Satan, seeing Noah planting the first vineyard, foresaw interesting possibilities. He immediately suggested that he and Noah become partners. When Noah agreed, Satan concluded the deal immediately. To symbolize the pact he slaughtered a lamb, a lion, a monkey, and a pig in that order and spilled their blood on the ground. Thus, when a man drinks just a little too much wine he becomes as sleepy as a lamb; when he drinks more, he becomes as fearless as a lion, still more and he begins jumping and gamboling about like a monkey, and when he drinks to surfeit he becomes as repugnant as a pig (*Tanhuma, Noah* 13). In another rabbinic passage two reasons are given why wine is red: (1) when a person realizes what he has done while inebriated, he blushes with shame; and (2) when one is under the influence of wine he may even come to shed blood.

It is thus clear that our Sages were aware that the drinking of wine can be harmful. And yet they bid us to begin each Sabbath with *Kiddush* over wine. This teaches us that the world is not divided into good and bad or holy and profane, but rather into good and not-yet-good, into holy and not-yet-holy. Wine when drunk with moderation can be an instrument for holiness. When abused, it becomes a source of harm and even tragedy. While everything is potentially dangerous, all of creation emanates from the Divine. The Jew is not to shun the physical; his task is to make it sacred, to sanctify every aspect of creation, to suffuse the physical with the spiritual potential in all things and, thus, make them holy.

A great teacher, Rav Moshe Poleyoff, once explained the difference between drinking for the sake of the mitzvah and drinking that leads to drunkenness. If one is empty inside and expects the wine to supply the happiness, the wine only leads to hopeless abandon and drunkenness. But if one is filled with joy and wishes to express that joy through drink, then the wine represents a *simhah shel mitzvah*—and the consumption of the wine itself becomes a mitzvah. That is the kind of drinking that takes place at the Passover Seder.

The Sanctity of Time

Every ancient people held certain places and objects sacred. The Jewish people, however, attached the most importance to sanctifying time. The Torah reserves blessing and sanctification not for the physical objects of creation but for the Sabbath: "And God blessed the Sabbath day and sanctified it" (Gen. 2:3)—it became an oasis of holy time.

The Kotzker Rebbe and the Vorker Rebbe once discussed the relative holiness of certain particular mitzvot. The Vorker observed that on Sukkot one chooses the four species after painstaking care to ensure their perfection and beauty. They are admired and waved, but finally they are laid aside, the commandment concerning them having been fulfilled. This is the way it is with most mitzvot: as long as we hold them we encompass the holy; the moment we release them the holiness departs. But when the Jew sits in the *sukkah*, he is surrounded by the commandment. The holy literally encompasses the Jew. Thus, *sukkah* is the greatest mitzvah. The Kotzker replied that the commandment concerning the Sabbath is even greater. The Jew can walk out of the *sukkah*, but he cannot walk out of the Sabbath. In other words, the sanctification of time is the ultimate sanctity, and since life is measured in time, holiness of time means holiness of life.

It is, thus, characteristic that the first commandment God gave the people of Israel as a nation—while yet in Egypt—was a mitzvah dealing with an aspect of time: "This month shall be to you the first of the months" (Ex. 12:1). The Torah clearly emphasizes our role in transforming and ennobling the time we are granted by the Almighty.

As Jews, we must view time not merely as objective, disparate units, such as minutes, days, etc., but rather as subjective, interconnected moments which we are empowered to fill with content and to sanctify with meaning. This idea is halakhically manifested in the institution of *kiddush ha-hodesh*, which is the process whereby we declare a certain day to be the beginning of the month. Originally the Great Sanhedrin, after hearing testimony from witnesses concerning the new moon, would proclaim the onset of a new month by the formula מְקוּדָּשׁ הַחוֹדֶשׁ, מְקוּדָּשׁ הַחוֹדֶשׁ ("the month is holy, the month is holy"). The court's decision determined on what day the festivals would occur. In contrast to the Sabbath, which occurs every seven days regardless of the calendar, the festivals depend on the determination of the month, which in turn is fixed by the Jewish people.

As Rabbi Ovadiah Sforno (ca. 1475–1550) observes in his Bible commentary, it is no coincidence that this commandment to sanctify time was given at the moment of freedom from Egypt. Slaves have no clear notion of time since it is not theirs to dispose of. Only free men, who have at least limited control over their time, can fill it with significant matters—and sanctify it. Thus, the concept of freedom and the sanctification of time are bound up with each other.

Universalism vs. Particularism

The first month in the Jewish calendar is the month of Nisan, the time of the emergence of the Jewish people. The seventh month is the month of Tishrei, the anniversary of the creation of man. The major Jewish holidays occur in or near these two major periods: Passover and Shavuot in the former; Rosh Hashanah, Yom Kippur, and Sukkot in the latter. The first group of holidays is characterized by its emphasis on the particular—on historical events of relevance only to the Jewish people, namely, emancipation from Egyptian bondage and the revelation at Mount Sinai. The holidays of the second group, however, contain universal themes and occur appropriately in the month when man was created.

Despite the fact that there is tension between particularism and universalism, between chauvinism and cosmopolitanism, both are part of the Jew's life-cycle. That they can be reconciled is an important motif of the *Kiddush*. By making reference in this blessing to both the creation of the world and the Exodus from Egypt, we affirm that there is no conflict between the two.

The Bible opens with the Lord of the Universe creating a world designed for all humanity and with instructions applicable to every individual. After the major Divine disappointments, first in Adam, then in Noah, the Almighty decides, as it were, to create a family out of which would be forged a "holy nation and kingdom of priests." This nation would by its example inspire the world to accept God's teachings. Hence at the very moment of his election, Abraham is promised by God that "all the families of the earth shall be blessed" through him. From the elevation of a particular people will follow the elevation of an entire peoplehood.

Thus, the calendar moves from Nisan, from the month representing our own national concerns, to the month of Tishrei, which symbolizes the universal, the needs of all nations. This progression reflects the concept that the Jews as a people achieve their full function—in the ultimate sense—when their efforts result in bringing perfection to all people. Kabbalistically speaking, the redemption comes when the world—including all its inhabitants—attains fullness and completion. This notion is alluded to in the Hebrew word שֶׁבַע, which means "seven" (Tishrei is the seventh month) and is symbolic of completion, for the world was created in seven days. The same Hebrew consonants when vocalized differently are read as שָׂבֵעַ, meaning "satiated" or "full." Satiation can come only when the world is complete in the sense that it is restored to God. We shall see more of this movement from nation to world in the *Hallel* psalms and in the entire development of the Passover Seder.

When the Seder night coincides with the Sabbath, we begin the *Kiddush* by reciting the portion of the Torah which describes God's resting on the seventh day. This in turn is followed by the festival *Kiddush* rather than the Sabbath *Kiddush*. While the latter emphasizes the relationship of the Sabbath to God and His cessation of work on the seventh day, the former refers to the Jewish people and their unique relationship with God as expressed through the holidays.

Havdalah   הַבְדָּלָה

If the first night of Passover falls on Saturday night, then the festival *Kiddush* is followed by *Havdalah*. Although logically we should say farewell to the Sabbath first through *Havdalah* and then usher in the festival with *Kiddush*, we do the reverse. Since the holiness of the Sabbath is greater than that of the holidays, we must show it greater love and reverence. To allow the Sabbath to depart slowly and with honor—to show that we long for it—the festival is greeted before the Sabbath is officially concluded, and therefore *Kiddush* precedes *Havdalah*.

In the *Havdalah* prayer we bless and thank God for having created various kinds of distinctions: between the holy and the secular, between light and darkness, between Israel and the nations, between the seventh day and the six days of toil, and finally between the holiness of the Sabbath and the holiness of the festival.

The last distinction, בֵּין קֹדֶשׁ לְקֹדֶשׁ (between "the holy and the holy"), requires some clarification. One tends to contrast it with the distinction between "the holy and the secular," which appears rather easy to make. However, on a kabbalistic level, neither of the two distinctions is facile, for everything in the world emanates from God's hand, and thus there is nothing that is without intrinsic holiness. The fact that distinctions must be made does not mean that the secular is condemned to perdition. It is up to man, by hallowing every day and every thing and by bringing them back to the service of God, to liberate the sparks of holiness inherent—or trapped—in every atom of creation. The word *hol,* as in *hol ha-moed,* means "empty"; it does not mean "profane." There exist the holy and the still-empty-of-holiness, the holy and the not-yet-holy, which is waiting for us to express its inherent sanctity. Thus, even to distinguish between the holy and the secular requires knowledge and perspicacity.

Now to "the holy and the holy." This phrase obviously refers to the contrast in holiness between the Sabbath and the festivals. How are they different conceptually? Shabbat celebrates the relationship between man and God. We acknowledge the Almighty as Creator of heaven and earth; our attention remains riveted upon God, and we thank Him for having given us a day on which we can rejoice in His kingdom. On the festivals, however, we emphasize (in our prayers and in the *Kiddush*) the relationship of the individual Jew to the people Israel. We rejoice in being part of the chosen people—chosen by God to carry out His divine mission.

Shabbat has very little to do with peoplehood. It is built into the very fabric of creation of the world and was sanctified before the existence of a Jewish nation. However, there could be no *yamim tovim,* no festivals, without a Jewish people. The festivals are milestones of Jewish history, days of remembrance of Israel's covenantal relationship with God, testimonies to the eternity of the Jewish nation.

On the basis of this conceptual distinction, we can better understand some of the halakhic differences between the Sabbath and the festivals. First, some of the acts of work that are forbidden on the Sabbath are permitted on the holidays. Most activities involving food preparation are permitted in one form or another on the latter. So too is the carrying of non-*muktzah* objects from place to place. Maimonides explains that the difference is due to the festival's being primarily a day of rejoicing whereas the Sabbath is characterized more as a day of sanctity. There cannot be complete joy without allowing food preparation or the carrying of certain essential items. Our conceptualization gives further meaning to the halakhic differences. We have a right to rejoice on the festivals since we—as the Jewish people—were partners with God in their creation; without the Jewish people there would be no holidays to celebrate our history. This is not true of the Sabbath, which predated the nation and is fundamentally a day of thanksgiving and recognition of God as the sole Creator of the universe.

Second, the very commandment to rejoice (וְשָׂמַחְתָּ) is limited to festivals. Shabbat, on the other hand, carries with it the obligation of *oneg*, which is different from *simḥah*. One of the practical results of this distinction is in the area of mourning. Since a Jew is enjoined to rejoice on the festival, he is forbidden to mourn during the holiday period. On the Sabbath, on the other hand, although any public display of mourning is forbidden, personal sadness and private acts of mourning are in order. Here again we can bring to bear our theory. Acts of mourning and despair contradict the spirit of the festivals, which symbolize the immortality of the Jewish people. The joy of the eternity of *Am Yisrael* overshadows the sadness at the loss of *Reb Yisrael*; the feelings of the many have priority over those of the few. Indeed, the communal character of the festival is brought home by the obligation upon the Jew to share his joy (and food) with "the stranger, the orphan, and the widow within your gates" (Deut. 16:11). The Sabbath, however, does not contain within it to the same extent the notion of joy or of communal participation, and, therefore, private mourning observance does not conflict with the spirit of the Sabbath.

In summation, God sanctifies the Sabbath, Israel sanctifies the festivals; God appointed the Sabbath, Israel declares when the festivals will fall—and God accepts Israel's decision. The Sabbath is God-centered, the festivals are Israel-centered. Both are holy, but with different kinds of holiness.

The Chosen People

The *Kiddush* proclaims in most elegant terms the praise of the Jewish people. It does so by emphasizing Israel's chosenness. This is a concept that is often misunderstood by gentiles—as well as by Jews.

The chosenness of Israel and its designation as a holy people—at least as understood and interpreted by Maimonides—are based solely upon its observance of God's commandments. There is no inherent notion of superiority—genetic or otherwise—in Israel's being the chosen people. The Jews were chosen for special responsibility and obligation, not for special privileges. Instructive is Maurice Samuel's response to the anti-Semitic jingle, "How odd of God to choose the Jews": "It was not at all odd; the Jews chose God." Because the Jews recognized and acknowledged the Almighty, He favored them as His people and chose them to carry out the mission to teach His ways to the world.

This concept lies behind the famous midrashic legend that just before the Revelation at Sinai, God went from nation to nation asking each to accept His Torah. The response was always the same: what was in the Torah? When God mentioned "Thou shalt not commit adultery" or "Thou shalt not steal," each nation rejected the Torah because it was not ready to accept such restrictions. When the Almighty offered the Torah to Israel, it declared without inquiry, *Na'aseh ve-nishmah*—"we shall do and [then] we shall understand." Because Israel chose God and His Torah, the Almighty chose Israel (see *Avodah Zarah* 2b and parallel passages).

Chosenness for the people of Israel has not been an unadulterated boon. Indeed much of our suffering can be attributed in part to this special status. Besides the enmity and envy engendered by this label among the gentiles throughout history, we have suffered by not living up to the responsibilities that attend the notion of chosenness. Thus the prophet Amos proclaimed: "Only you have I loved from all the families of the earth; therefore do I visit upon you all of your sins" (Amos 3:2). The price Israel pays for Divine revelation is its responsibility to live up to it.

Nevertheless, if there is any concept which has maintained Jewish identity throughout the generations, it is this notion of our Divine election. Mendele Mokher Seforim (1835–1917) tells a poignant story of a Jewish dairyman, a *milchiker*, who was traveling with his little son in a broken-down wagon drawn by a very hungry horse. As they travel, the father attempts to teach his son Bible, but the youth seems far more interested in the passing scenery than in the Hebrew verses of the text. Suddenly the magnificent carriage of the *poretz*, the landowner, drawn by two magnificent horses, thunders by in a cloud of choking dust. The *poretz* himself, big-bellied, well-fed, well-dressed, rings covering his fingers, an expensive watch in his vest pocket, smoking a big cigar, sits in the back. The Jew, in tattered, torn clothing, turns in desperation to his son and exclaims, "I want you to learn Torah because, God forbid, if you don't, you will look like that gentile over there." No matter what the world thought about the Jews, they reveled in the belief that they were closer to the Almighty.

James Baldwin once wrote that he might be able to forgive whites for persecuting blacks but will never forgive them for making blacks feel inferior. In two thousand years of persecution, pogrom, and exile, we Jews never allowed ourselves to feel inferior. We always believed that we were the bearers of God's law. No idea played a more important role in protecting our national pride and our unique destiny.

She-heheyanu   שֶׁהֶחֱיָנוּ

The Abudarham (Rabbi David b. Joseph Abudarham, 14th century), most famous for his commentary on the prayerbook, asked why we recite the *she-heheyanu* blessing on the festivals but not on the Sabbath. He answered that *she-heheyanu* is said for anything that is anxiously expected or eagerly anticipated, such as every week or month. Thus, *she-heheyanu* is not recited on the Sabbath—or even on Rosh Hodesh. In the Midrash, the Sabbath with its greater frequency is metaphorically compared to a wife, while the festivals are likened to a bride. To be sure, one awaits a bride with greater anticipation. As to love, however, it is the more constant and loyal wife who has the greater claim. So too the Sabbath, while awaited with less eagerness than the festivals, nevertheless is more holy and, therefore, the object of greater love.

Is there a conceptual difference between *hayyim* (''life'') and *kiyyum* (''existence'')? Or are these words synonyms for the same concept? From Targum Onkelos to Deuteronomy 8:3, we can infer that the two terms represent different ideas. The oft-cited verse reads in translation: ''Not by bread alone does the human being live (יִחְיֶה הָאָדָם), but by all that comes forth from the mouth of God does he live (יִחְיֶה הָאָדָם).'' While the Bible uses the same term יִחְיֶה הָאָדָם in both parts of this coordinate clause, the Targum translation gives it two different Aramaic renderings. In the first instance, which contains the reference to bread, it has מִתְקַיַּם אֱנָשָׁא (the human being *exists*), but in the second instance it has חַיֵי אֱנָשָׁא (the human being *lives*).° Onkelos' shift from מִתְקַיַּם to חַיֵי is due no doubt to the difference between the two sources of life referred to in the verse. While bread supports an earthy, physical existence (= קִיּוּם), it is the Torah, or that which comes from the mouth of God, which sustains an elevated, spiritual life (= חַיִּים).

Man is certainly a physical being whose requirements are no different from those of any animal: food, drink, rest, etc. Thus he needs *kiyyum*. But the human being requires more; he needs life with meaning, purpose, and a goal. Victor Frankl, the Viennese psychoanalyst and founder of logotherapy, showed that the most important drive in modern man is not pleasure or power, but the search for meaning. Frankl learned from his experiences in a Nazi concentration camp that a human being can take virtually any amount of physical torture as long as he feels it is for some higher purpose. What sustained many of our people in the barbaric conditions of those camps was: (1) their hope that the miserable conditions would soon end and that meaningful life would be resumed, and (2) their belief that somehow their plight served a Divine plan—that it was not for nought.

Meaning, purpose, and goal are essentially what we ask for during the Ten Days of Penitence between Rosh Hashanah and Yom

° So Berliner's ed. of Targum Onkelos (Berlin, 1884), but some versions have מתקים (or derivatives thereof) for both. Cf. נְתִינָה לַגֵּר *ad loc.*

Kippur. The Berdichever Rebbe gave a novel interpretation to the prayer of זָכְרֵנוּ, which we recite in each *Amidah* during the Ten Days. Instead of reading וְכָתְבֵנוּ בְּסֵפֶר הַחַיִּים לְמַעַנְךָ אֱלֹקִים חַיִּים, with a pause between הַחַיִּים and לְמַעַנְךָ (meaning "Write us into the Book of Life, for Your sake, O God of life"), he suggested that we should read the words הַחַיִּים לְמַעַנְךָ without a pause between them. We are thus praying to God not merely for life but for life for His sake. We

Everyone at the table has a glass or cup of wine before him.

קַדֵּשׁ

כּוֹס רִאשׁוֹנָה

הִנְנִי מוּכָן וּמְזֻמָּן לְקַיֵּם מִצְוַת כּוֹס רִאשׁוֹנָה מֵאַרְבַּע כּוֹסוֹת לְשֵׁם יִחוּד קוּדְשָׁא בְּרִיךְ־הוּא וּשְׁכִינְתֵּיה עַל־יְדֵי הַהוּא טָמִיר וְנֶעְלָם בְּשֵׁם כָּל־יִשְׂרָאֵל.

If the festival is on Friday night, the following is added:

וַיְהִי־עֶרֶב וַיְהִי־בֹקֶר

יוֹם הַשִּׁשִּׁי: וַיְכֻלּוּ, הַשָּׁמַיִם וְהָאָרֶץ וְכָל־צְבָאָם: וַיְכַל אֱלֹהִים בַּיּוֹם הַשְּׁבִיעִי, מְלַאכְתּוֹ אֲשֶׁר עָשָׂה, וַיִּשְׁבֹּת בַּיּוֹם הַשְּׁבִיעִי, מִכָּל־מְלַאכְתּוֹ אֲשֶׁר עָשָׂה: וַיְבָרֶךְ אֱלֹהִים אֶת־יוֹם הַשְּׁבִיעִי, וַיְקַדֵּשׁ אֹתוֹ, כִּי בוֹ שָׁבַת מִכָּל־מְלַאכְתּוֹ, אֲשֶׁר־בָּרָא אֱלֹהִים לַעֲשׂוֹת:

If the festival is on another night of the week, begin here: (On the Sabbath add words in parentheses.)

סַבְרִי מָרָנָן וְרַבָּנָן וְרַבּוֹתַי:

בָּרוּךְ אַתָּה יְיָ, אֱלֹהֵינוּ מֶלֶךְ הָעוֹלָם, בּוֹרֵא פְּרִי הַגָּפֶן:

ask for life that has meaning beyond physical existence. It is not life for life's sake that we want, but life for God's sake.

To summarize, we thank God in the *she-heḥeyanu* blessing for giving us *ḥayyim*, which is meaningful, fulfilling life, and for *kiyyum*—basic physical existence. The blessing concludes with thanksgiving for having reached this special time of the Passover Seder.

Everyone at the table has a glass or cup of wine before him.

KADESH

THE FIRST CUP

If the festival is on Friday night, the following is added:

And it was evening and it was morning.
The sixth day. The heavens, the earth, and all their hosts were finished. God declared complete on the seventh day the work which He had done, and He rested on the seventh day from all His work which He had done. And God blessed the seventh day and made it holy, because on it He rested from all His work which He had done in creation.

If the festival is on another night of the week, begin here: (On the Sabbath add words in parentheses.)

Blessed art Thou, Eternal our God, Ruler of the universe, Creator of the fruit of the vine.

בָּרוּךְ אַתָּה יְיָ, אֱלֹהֵינוּ מֶלֶךְ הָעוֹלָם, אֲשֶׁר בָּחַר בָּנוּ מִכָּל־עָם, וְרוֹמְמָנוּ
מִכָּל־לָשׁוֹן, וְקִדְּשָׁנוּ בְּמִצְוֹתָיו, וַתִּתֶּן לָנוּ יְיָ אֱלֹהֵינוּ בְּאַהֲבָה (לשבת
שַׁבָּתוֹת לִמְנוּחָה וּ) מוֹעֲדִים לְשִׂמְחָה, חַגִּים וּזְמַנִּים לְשָׂשׂוֹן, אֶת־יוֹם
(לשבת הַשַּׁבָּת הַזֶּה, וְאֶת־יוֹם) חַג־הַמַּצּוֹת הַזֶּה. זְמַן חֵרוּתֵנוּ, (לשבת
בְּאַהֲבָה) מִקְרָא קֹדֶשׁ, זֵכֶר לִיצִיאַת מִצְרָיִם. כִּי בָנוּ בָחַרְתָּ, וְאוֹתָנוּ
קִדַּשְׁתָּ, מִכָּל־הָעַמִּים. (לשבת וְשַׁבָּת) וּמוֹעֲדֵי קָדְשֶׁךָ (לשבת בְּאַהֲבָה
וּבְרָצוֹן) בְּשִׂמְחָה וּבְשָׂשׂוֹן הִנְחַלְתָּנוּ: בָּרוּךְ אַתָּה יְיָ, מְקַדֵּשׁ (לשבת הַשַּׁבָּת
וְ) יִשְׂרָאֵל וְהַזְּמַנִּים:

If the festival is not on Saturday night, recite she-heheyanu here.
(See below)

If the festival falls on Saturday night, add the following:

בָּרוּךְ אַתָּה יְיָ, אֱלֹהֵינוּ מֶלֶךְ הָעוֹלָם, בּוֹרֵא מְאוֹרֵי הָאֵשׁ:

בָּרוּךְ אַתָּה יְיָ אֱלֹהֵינוּ מֶלֶךְ הָעוֹלָם, הַמַּבְדִּיל בֵּין קֹדֶשׁ לְחוֹל, בֵּין אוֹר
לְחֹשֶׁךְ, בֵּין יִשְׂרָאֵל לָעַמִּים, בֵּין יוֹם הַשְּׁבִיעִי לְשֵׁשֶׁת יְמֵי הַמַּעֲשֶׂה. בֵּין
קְדֻשַׁת שַׁבָּת לִקְדֻשַׁת יוֹם טוֹב הִבְדַּלְתָּ. וְאֶת־יוֹם הַשְּׁבִיעִי מִשֵּׁשֶׁת יְמֵי
הַמַּעֲשֶׂה קִדַּשְׁתָּ. הִבְדַּלְתָּ וְקִדַּשְׁתָּ אֶת־עַמְּךָ יִשְׂרָאֵל בִּקְדֻשָּׁתֶךָ: בָּרוּךְ
אַתָּה יְיָ, הַמַּבְדִּיל בֵּין קֹדֶשׁ לְקֹדֶשׁ:

בָּרוּךְ אַתָּה יְיָ, אֱלֹהֵינוּ מֶלֶךְ הָעוֹלָם, שֶׁהֶחֱיָנוּ, וְקִיְּמָנוּ, וְהִגִּיעָנוּ, לַזְּמַן
הַזֶּה:

Leaning on the left side, drink the first cup of wine.

Blessed art Thou, Eternal our god, Ruler of the universe, Who chose us from all peoples and exalted us among all nations, by making us holy with His commandments. With love You gave us (the Sabbath for rest, and) the festivals for happiness, holidays and seasons for rejoicing; as this day (of Sabbath, and this day) of the Feast of Matzot, the season of our freedom, which is a holy assembly, in remembrance of the going out from Egypt. For You have chosen us from all peoples to make us holy with (the Sabbath and) Your holy festivals (with love and favor) in joy and in happiness. Blessed art Thou, Who makes holy (the Sabbath and) Israel and the festive seasons.

If the festival is not on Saturday night, recite she-heheyanu here. (See below)

If the festival falls on Saturday night, add the following:

Blessed art Thou, Eternal our God, Ruler of the universe, Creator of light and fire.

Blessed art Thou, Eternal our God, Ruler of the universe, Who makes a distinction between the holy and the plain, between light and darkness, between Israel and the other nations, between the seventh day and the six days of work. You have made a distinction between the holiness of the Sabbath and the holiness of the festivals, and You made the seventh day holier than the six days of work. You have distinguished and made holy Your people Israel with Your holiness. Blessed art Thou, Who makes a distinction between holiness and holiness.

Blessed art Thou, Eternal our God, Ruler of the universe, Who has given us life and sustenance and brought us to this happy season.

Leaning on the left side, drink the first cup of wine.

THE WASHING OF HANDS   וּרְחַץ

The Seder is a re-creation of a moment in history—a glimpse into our past. In the drama of the Seder night we reexperience not only the Exodus from Egypt but also the ways in which the Jewish people have celebrated this event throughout their history, especially when the Temple stood and the Jews were in the Holy Land. At that time Jews would go up to Jerusalem to slaughter the paschal lamb as an offering on the altar and to partake of its meat on the night of the Seder. The males regarded themselves as priests dedicated to the service of the Almighty. The *kittel*, the white robe worn by the male celebrants at the Seder, represents the priestly garb worn during the sacrificial service at the Holy Temple.

Another feature that recalls the ancient past is the washing of the hands following *Kiddush*, what we call *urhatz*. While Halakhah demands that we ritually wash our hands with a blessing before partaking of bread, in Temple times other foods also required, under certain conditions, the washing of one's hands. In particular, fruits and vegetables were subject to ritual defilement once they came into contact with water. To guard against any impurity, the Rabbis instituted the ritual washing of hands prior to eating such foods. At the Passover Seder we conduct ourselves as we did when we had the Temple, and we perform the ritual washing before partaking of the vegetable dipped in salt water—but we do so without the customary blessing. By this act we also express our hope that the Holy Temple will be rebuilt speedily—even within our lifetime—and that complete redemption will come to the world.

URHATZ   וּרְחַץ

Wash your hands, but do not say the blessing. A cup of water is taken in the left hand, and half of it is poured twice over the right hand. Then the other half is poured twice over the left hand.

KARPAS   כַּרְפַּס

The vegetable that we dip into salt water is the *karpas*. The name is derived from the Greek word for "grass" or "vegetation." By Divine mandate, Passover is the spring festival and must be celebrated *be-tekufat ha-aviv* (Deut. 16:1), when the greenery begins to sprout. It is more than a coincidence that the birth of the Jewish people and the rebirth of all of nature take place in the same month.

Parsley is generally used for *karpas*, but other kinds of green vegetables are permitted. The green color reminds us of the onset of spring when the fields are verdant. The salt water into which we dip the *karpas* symbolizes the tears the Israelites shed in Egypt.

On a more prosaic level, *karpas*, as the Greek etymology indicates, represents the ancient Greco-Roman custom of beginning the meal with a vegetable hors d'oeuvre replete with a dipping. On Seder night we are no longer slaves, but we emulate the customs of "high society" by eating a vegetable *vorspeis* while we recline on our divans.

Eating — A Religious Experience

The Talmud attaches added meaning to the dipping of the *karpas* in salt water by explaining it as a ploy to get the children to ask questions. One might wonder why this particular means was chosen to arouse the children's curiosity. One could have stimulated them to ask questions by decorating the table with colored balloons or by standing on one's head. It is apparent then that the ritual of *karpas* and salt water is intended to provoke the young to ask certain specific questions whose answers we, as parents, are waiting to give. One of these questions, as we shall elaborate, goes to the heart of the issue of how man is different from any other living being.

The Torah teaches a person to attain his daily physical needs in a human way—not as an animal. For example, the way a human being eats should be different from the manner in which an animal consumes its food. Man may not sit down at a table and fall upon his food. He must first recite a blessing to indicate that the food serves a higher goal. It becomes a vehicle to serve the Creator. Man eats in a dignified manner and afterwards offers a prayer of thanks to the Provider of the food. Not so the beast! The hungry animal hunts its food, eats it at once, continues without interruption until it is satiated, and goes away. The animal eats only to still its hunger; it has no sense of restraint.

The Torah characterizes Esau as a beast-man. When he grew up he became a skillful hunter, while his brother, Jacob, remained a scholar, who stayed behind to tend the sheep. Once when Jacob was cooking a stew, Esau came in from the fields famished, according to the Bible, and demanded some food. Jacob fed Esau bread and lentil soup, and "he ate, drank, rose, and went away" (Gen. 25:34). The Rabbis observed that there was no washing of hands, no beginning prayer, and no *birkat ha-mazon*. This is how a beast eats.

The Seder can serve as a model to teach us the Jewish philosophy of eating. We observe that we permit ourselves to have only a tiny portion of *karpas*. By immediately withdrawing from the food, we learn discipline and restraint. As human beings we must learn the self-control to put the food aside and make of the meal a religious experience. By learning to do not what we have the urge to do, but what He commands, we serve God.

For the Jew the meal is a religious experience that also serves a social function. It binds the family and the community to each other, to their common past, and to their common future, as well as to their God. The food is secondary; the most important element of the meal is what is the spiritual component—that which emerges from the דִּבְרֵי תּוֹרָה (words of Torah) that are exchanged.

Hence the Seder begins by our drinking a cup of wine together and having a *vorspeis* of greenery, and then, just when we would expect the food to arrive, we stop eating. The children will wonder, "What is going on? This is strange. We did not eat much lunch because of the great Seder dinner. Now, where is the food?" The parents will respond by telling of the special character of Passover. On that holiday we became a people of God whose primary purpose is to serve Him. We do so by subsuming the physical to the spiritual—by turning a meal into a learning experience and a prayer experience. Indeed the learning and prayer come first. It is through *karpas* that this lesson is brought home to the children at the Seder table.

A charming story is told about two beggars, Yidel, a Jew, and Ivan, a Russian. Both were always in need of a good meal, and one year, just before Passover, Yidel told Ivan that if he went into a synagogue and pretended to be a Jew, he would be sure to get an invitation to a Seder. About a month later, when they met once again, Yidel expected an embrace and a thank-you, but instead Ivan fell upon him with blows and curses. Finally he explained. "I did exactly what you said. I went to the synagogue, sat in the last row, did everything the others did, and played the deaf-mute. I got about a dozen invitations and went with the man who looked to be the richest. The table was set beautifully and his house was full of the aroma of cooked food. I sat down and waited to be served, but first they began chanting in Hebrew. After a while they gave me a cup of wine and some parsley and salt water. A strange dish but edible. Meanwhile they kept on swaying and reading Hebrew. I was almost faint with hunger. Ten minutes, twenty minutes, an hour passed. I thought I would go mad. At last everyone got up and washed their hands. So did I. Then they gave me a flat, tasteless wafer and passed around a vegetable I had never seen before. I took a huge bite, and all of a sudden my eyes started to tear. I began to choke and my insides were burning. They must have known that I was a goy. So I ran from the table. I'm sure you put them up to it." "Oh, my friend," said Yidel. "If only you'd been a little more patient. After the *karpas*, matzah, and *maror*, all the delicious food would have come." This is really what a Seder is: a great deal of reading, a great deal of swaying to and fro, a great deal of talking and learning. It requires much patience, but a meal par excellence for a Jew consists of far more than food.

KARPAS   כַּרְפַּס

The master of the house then takes some parsley, or any green vegetable, and dips it into vinegar or salt water, and when it is distributed to everyone at the table, they say the following blessing before eating it:

Blessed art Thou, Eternal our God, Ruler of the universe, Creator of the fruit of the earth.

בָּרוּךְ אַתָּה יְיָ, אֱלֹהֵינוּ מֶלֶךְ הָעוֹלָם, בּוֹרֵא פְּרִי הָאֲדָמָה:

The Paradox of the Seder

The middle matzah is broken into two pieces of which one is used later to fulfill the mitzvah of eating matzah. The reason a broken piece is used is that matzah is a symbol of affliction, especially when broken. On the first night of Pesach we are obligated to eat *lehem oni*, which is usually translated as "bread of affliction." It is the "bread" that our fathers ate in Egypt. Matzah is bread that "did not make it." It is the kind of food that is put together by a slave who has not the leisure to allow the dough to rise.

Interestingly, matzah is also the symbol of redemption. It is the food that our ancestors ate while leaving Egypt in haste. The dough had no time to rise, because the time of redemption had come and there could be no delay. The Zohar refers to the matzah as לַחְמָא דִמְהֵימְנוּתָא—the "bread of faith." It represents the faith of Israel in God as our Redeemer.

The Seder is thus filled with paradox. It makes you feel the servitude as well as the redemption, the sorrow as well as the exultation.

One might wonder why we break off a piece of matzah now at the very beginning of the Seder rather than later at the time of the blessing when we actually eat it. The simple answer is that we need the broken piece throughout the Seder while we describe the redemption as a visible symbol of the *lehem oni* our fathers ate in Egypt. On a deeper level, the very act of breaking a piece of "bread" in two and saving for later demonstrates its character as *lehem oni*. Only a poor person who does not know when or if his next meal will come breaks off from what he has now and saves it for later. Since most of us do not know what poverty is, we begin the Seder by becoming acquainted with it, at least symbolically. We declare that this matzah is the bread of poverty that our fathers ate at various stages of history, and we break a piece off and save it for later as they used to do.

In the messianic sense, the piece we save for later symbolizes the Leviathan meal—the sumptuous repast at which God Himself will serve the righteous the fish and meat of the mystical Leviathan and Behemoth. The matzah will serve as a dessert at that great Seder when the Messiah will have come and the world will no longer know of famine and poverty.

Three Matzot or Two?

There is debate among the halakhic authorities as to how many matzot should be displayed on the Seder dish. The generally accepted custom is to use three, with the middle matzah to be broken. Some, however, in accordance with the opinion of the Vilna Gaon (1720–1797), make use of two matzot, with the lower one to be broken.

The controversy over the number of matzot has its roots in the Talmud and the Rishonim. Let us examine the passage in *Pesaḥim* which bears upon this issue (*Pes.* 115b). There we find two opinions offered on the meaning of *leḥem oni,* which is a biblical epithet for matzah (Deut. 16:3). Shmuel teaches that it is called *leḥem oni* because it is the bread upon which we sing many songs during the Seder (i.e., deriving עוֹנִי from עוֹנִין). Others say it is called *leḥem oni* because only a broken piece of matzah is used to fulfill the mitz- vah, just as a poor person has to suffice with less than a whole matzah (i.e., deriving עוֹנִי from עָנִי).

As to the nature of the matzah or matzot used, we have R. Papa's statement (*Berakhot* 39b): "All agree that on Passover one places the broken piece under the whole [and makes a blessing thereon] since the Torah calls it the 'bread of affliction.'" To this R. Abba adds: "On the Sabbath one must say *ha-motzi* over two whole loaves since the Torah uses the term לֶחֶם מִשְׁנֶה in reference to the Sabbath provisions." Assuming that the festivals are like the Sabbath and *leḥem mishneh* is required, how does one fulfill this obligation on the Seder night?

Rashi (*Pesaḥim* 116a) maintains that the broken piece of matzah must be accompanied by two whole matzot. While the blessing of עַל אֲכִילַת מַצָּה is recited over the half piece, the blessing of הַמּוֹצִיא must be made over two whole matzot, as Passover is not inferior to the Sabbath and other holidays. In contrast to Rashi, Maimonides writes (Laws of Leavened and Unleavened Bread 8:6) that only two matzot, one whole and one broken, are used for the two blessings.

Rashi's opinion appears to be the more logical, for he allows—by the use of three matzot—the realization of both לֶחֶם עוֹנִי and לֶחֶם מִשְׁנֶה. Maimonides' position seems to be less tenable—and even problematic—for he allows no fulfillment of לֶחֶם מִשְׁנֶה on Passover. Surely it should be no different in this respect from the other festivals!

The solution lies perhaps in Rambam's understanding of the special meaning of Passover. While the other festivals commemorate something that is complete—for example, the Revelation at Sinai on Shavuot—the same is not true of Passover. On this holiday we celebrate the Almighty as a Redeemer, but complete redemption has not yet come. Jews are still in exile. Those behind the Iron Curtain still cannot eat matzah in freedom. In Iran and in Arab countries Jews are often in danger of their lives. All this must be expressed in our Seder and must temper the joy of our celebration. Because our redemption, and therefore our joy, is not complete, we cannot rejoice with the usual *lehem mishneh*.

Rabbi Nachman of Bratslav (1772–1811) once asked, "Who is a whole man? He who has a broken heart." As long as Israel is not yet fully redeemed, the second matzah must be broken. It remains as a reminder and symbol within the very festival of redemption that we are not yet redeemed.

YAḤATZ   יַחַץ

The master of the house breaks the middle matzah in the plate, and leaving the smaller half of it there, he puts aside the larger half till after dinner, for the afikoman.

MAGID

מַגִּיד

HA LAḤMA ANYA

הָא לַחְמָא עַנְיָא

We are now at the beginning of the essential Seder. *Kiddush* is common to all festivals, and *karpas* is the prologue, the *vorspeis.* With *yaḥatz* we demonstrate our affinity with the past—when we ourselves were slaves, when we indeed knew the taste of poverty. And now we look to others in similar straits. We call to the poor and downtrodden to join us—we who were also poor and friendless at one time.

Ha laḥma anya is an invitation for all to hear. Lifting up the matzah is not a dignified demonstration for the benefit of the guests at the Seder alone. It is a call to the street, to the ghetto, to the village, to the world that the poor need not despair. In the same spirit the prophet Isaiah shouted to the world, "Ho! All ye who thirst, come and drink from the living waters [of the Torah]" (Isa. 55:1).

But the statement *ha laḥma anya* goes deeper. The Seder meal is a meal par excellence that links us to each other, to God, and to our less-fortunate brethren. In a sense we reexperience our servitude in Egypt in order that we may never forget what it means to be a slave. We thus invite the poor and the hungry to join us, for as Jews we know full well what it means to be an outcast. We eat the "bread of affliction" to remind us of our past and to warn us that we are not yet fully redeemed. Folklore tells of a rich man who concluded each of his fine meals with a coarse piece of bread dipped in salt water in remembrance of the days of his affliction. Another story tells of a wealthy householder who frequently put on the clothes he had worn during his days of poverty. In time the man lost his wealth and was reduced to wearing his old, tattered clothes again. His children still respected him as their father and did not feel alienated from him after his sudden plunge into misfortune.

Even though we are not slaves anymore, we are never out of danger of being enslaved once again. The Holocaust is only one generation behind us. As Elie Wiesel has written: the nation that stood together at Sinai and heard the *anokhi* is the same nation that experienced Auschwitz together. Even should our safety and the trappings of affluence be stripped from us and we appear once again in the slave garb or the striped pajamas of the concentration camp, we know that God will not be alienated from us but will recognize us as His people. The Passover Seder reminds us that Israel was chosen when its fortunes were low; it will surely not be abandoned if the pendulum brings us back to such a state.

Every people of antiquity made great efforts to trace its ancestry back to heroes and gods. The Jewish people were different. They devoted a whole book of the Torah, and a good part of the Seder evening, to describing their origins in slavery and oppression, a fact that other nations would have covered with silence as an unspeakable shame. We fully believe that the Almighty destined this slave interlude to teach Israel as intensively as possible the meaning of slavery and the significance of redemption. The Torah returns again and again to the slave motif: Remember that you were a stranger in the Land of Egypt. Remembering our own slavery places us under the ethic of protecting and supporting the stranger, the slave, and the oppressed, and requires us to fight the inhuman and anti-human wherever we find it. To the Torah the oppression of the defenseless is a heinous evil. It is up to the Jewish people, who have experienced it in their selves, to extirpate it.

Hungry vs. Needy

Why do we distinguish between the hungry (דִּכְפִין) and the needy (דִּצְרִיךְ)? Are not the needy hungry? The answer might be that hunger does not mean only a lack of physical nourishment. It can mean hunger for human companionship and human concern. The abandonment of the lonely and the aged is one of the great problems of contemporary American society. However great the poverty, in the *shtetl* there was always companionship. Each family knew the problems of the other, and, knowing the pangs of hunger and the meaning of depression, was willing to help. In America there is little poverty among Jews, but we still allow the lonely and the aged to wither away alone. At best they are sent to nursing homes or to senior citizen residences, where they can be forgotten with smaller pangs of conscience. We generally prefer to write a check rather than face the poor directly, much less take them into our homes.

The "needy" are the pressured, the spiritually confused, the psychologically perplexed, the lonely, the aged—all those who have fallen beneath the wheels of our increasingly demanding and abrasive society. At the Seder we offer them an opportunity to share our redemptive experience so that they can take control of their daily lives once again. All of us need food for the body and food for the spirit; the Seder abundantly provides both.

The contrast between the hungry and the needy is masterfully and lovingly described in Shmuel Yosef Agnon's short story "The Passover Celebrants" (*Passover Anthology,* Jewish Publication Society, Philadelphia, 1966). Here is the bitterly poor *shammes* trudging home after evening services to an empty room, to a "Seder" made up only of the bare necessities for which he scrimped and saved for months. And there is the wealthy childless widow, who from force of habit has prepared the same marvelous Seder she always did when her husband was still alive. The Seder plate and the food are waiting on a table gleaming with silver and spotless linen, but the widow is alone and empty in soul and spirit. By chance she discovers the *shammes* on his way home and invites him to share the Seder with her. The time-honored words of the Haggadah and the old, familiar ritual blend into the most wonderful Seder for both of them, the hungry and the needy. At the conclusion, when the widow and the *shammes* recite the *Shir Ha-Shirim* together, there is hope that there will be no more hunger and loneliness at least for these Passover celebrants.

There are also people who have food and companionship but, having moved away from the glorious Jewish tradition, feel that their lives are empty and purposeless. They too are in need. Hence, we say, "Let anyone who is in need—in need of food, in need of companionship, in need of experiencing the glory of the Jewish tradition—come and spend Passover with us." The Seder is thus an opportunity to invite even those who have become estranged from the tradition and reunite them with their heritage.

The Disbeliever at the Seder

In our society the Seder has been so popularized that it is celebrated even in households where few rituals are observed. Occasionally even a Jew who professes no belief in God will find himself at a Seder. But does the participation of an agnostic (or even an atheist) have any particular religious value, or is it simply a hypocritical act which "makes no sense"?

This question is related to the wider issue of whether the observance of mitzvot is predicated upon belief in God. Stated otherwise, is belief in God the central, underlying basis for all of Judaism, or is it one particular mitzvah out of the 613, albeit a very important one? The Rishonim nearly a thousand years ago debated this issue in connection with the status of the first of the Ten Commandments, "I am the Lord thy God who took thee out of the Land of Egypt . . . ." Is this a separate mitzvah requiring belief in God, or is it simply a statement of fact? Most interesting is the view of Naḥmanides, who, to explain the omission of belief in God as one of the 613 mitzvot, proposes that this tenet of belief is more than just a commandment; it is the matrix from which all other commandments flow. The great medieval philosopher Ḥasdai Crescas (d. 1412) wrote in his treatise *Or Hashem* that to even mention the word *mitzvah* ("command") without predicating a *metzaveh* ("commander") is a logical absurdity. Thus, to return to our question, it would appear at the least incongruous to have an atheist or an agnostic participate in a religious ritual such as a Seder. Nevertheless, one can look upon the issue at hand from a different perspective—one that is commensurate with Rashi's interpretation of "I am the Lord thy God [who took thee out of the Land of Egypt, out of the house of bondage]." The commentator par excellence does not read this verse as a commandment, or as an introduction to the other commandments. To him it is a statement of experience. He has God saying to the Jewish people, "I am the Lord thy God— in all my manifestations to you I am the same God, viz., the One who brought you out of the Land of Egypt." Whether it be the warring God at the Red Sea or the teaching God at Mount Sinai, it is one and the same God.

For some Jews participation in the Seder is not due to belief in a God who commanded such participation. Rather, their involvement is due to the need to share in a common religious or even social experience or perhaps out of plain curiosity. These Jews are often seekers rather than finders. If they do find God it is not from the wellsprings of belief but from the meanderings of experience. While they may not accept the God of the Sinaitic revelation, they might discover the God of the Red Sea parting. It is one and the same God. We must, therefore, *not* discourage Jews who are agnostics, or even atheists, from joining with us at the Seder table. If they do not arrive at religious truth in one manner—through Torah—they may arrive at it in another manner—through history, through community, through the beauty of ritual. Let us recall that even the Wicked Son has his place at the Seder.

THE PASSOVER STORY   מַגִּיד

Uncover the matzah and lift up the plate for all to see. The recital of the Haggadah begins with the following words:

This is the bread of affliction which our forefathers ate in the land of Egypt. All who are hungry—let them come and eat. All who are needy—let them come and celebrate the Passover with us. Now we are here; next year may we be in the Land of Israel. Now we are slaves; next year may we be free men.

הָא לַחְמָא עַנְיָא, דִּי אֲכָלוּ אַבְהָתָנָא בְּאַרְעָא דְמִצְרָיִם. כָּל־דִּכְפִין יֵיתֵי וְיֵכוֹל, כָּל־דִּצְרִיךְ יֵיתֵי וְיִפְסַח. הָשַׁתָּא הָכָא, לְשָׁנָה הַבָּאָה בְּאַרְעָא דְיִשְׂרָאֵל. הָשַׁתָּא עַבְדֵי, לְשָׁנָה הַבָּאָה בְּנֵי חוֹרִין:

The plate is put down, the matzah is covered, and the second cup of wine is filled. The youngest present asks the Four Questions.

The Four Questions

Maggid has a dual purpose: to link us to the future as well as to the past. We must thrust into the future to remain human and not to despair. We communicate to our children (the future) the experience of the past in order to inform the present, and through them to shape our collective future. This is the goal of *maggid*.

What does *maggid* consist of? Questions and answers. There are two pedagogical principles that the Seder ritual—and all of Halakhah—presumes and that modern education has begun to recognize. First, you cannot make someone learn something he is not interested in knowing about. Second, you must experience with all five senses if you are to truly understand. The Seder takes into account these principles and accordingly provides the proper context for arousing a child's curiosity and interest and involving him totally in the ritual. As a result the child asks questions; he wants to learn and to experience.

To some extent the Haggadah should be imparted as a story, because children are not yet able to understand the philosophical implications. If Judaism were only a theology, one could not easily impart it to children. But Judaism is first and foremost an experience, and experience can and must be taught to young children. How do you teach a three-year-old child about Passover? Show him matzah; show him *maror*, the Seder dish, the wine, the special foods; and sing the joyous Passover songs. The story can be told in simple terms, but it is through symbols that the story becomes more vivid. The symbols encourage the questions, whether they be those of the three-year-old or those of the fifty-year-old.

The Mishnah teaches: "They pour the second cup of wine, and here the child asks the parent. If the child does not have the knowledge to ask, then his father prompts him with "מַה נִּשְׁתַּנָּה הַלַּיְלָה הַזֶּה (*Pesaḥim* 10:4). The מַה נִּשְׁתַּנָּה is simply a way of inspiring the youth. This mishnah makes it clear that the Four Questions should not be frozen into a formula or remain the only questions asked. Indeed we encourage the children—or adults—to ask many questions: questions about Jewish identity, the origins and the future of our people, Jewish law and history, the symbolism of the ritual, and questions about God and Jewish destiny. Jewish tradition is filled with the notion that the question is more important than the answer. No technical terms are more frequently found in the Talmud than the terms for questions. We are a people who have constantly questioned, and every good educator knows that he values a *gute kashe* ("good question") far more than any response. If you ask the right question, you will ultimately come upon the correct answers or the right solutions. Thus on this night we encourage the participants to ask and to question.

A great Hasidic Rebbe once asked why we insist on questions only on Passover night. Are there not aspects of other festivals and their rituals that are at least as strange as some of the Pesach rituals that evoke the Four Questions? Why do we not ask four questions on Sukkot, including one such as "On all other nights of the year we sit and eat in our home, but on this night we eat outside in a little hut"? At least four questions could certainly be asked about other Jewish festivals. The Rebbe answered his own query. For a Jew to have to leave his secure home and suddenly have to eat his meal in a small rickety hut is not a strange experience. That has been the story of the Jew's life for the last two thousand years and, unfortunately, does not raise a single question. For the Jews to sit around an opulent Seder table, however, is strange enough to warrant many questions. One might add to the Rebbe's words: For the Jew to thank God for his redemption when all of Jewish history seems to teach the opposite, occasions not only four questions but many more.

The Four Questions themselves reflect a curious paradox of servitude and redemption. The matzah, which is the subject of the first question, is a slave bread but also a symbol of freedom. We go on to the bitter herbs in the second question. They are a symbol of servitude, but their use as hors d'oeuvre and their being dipped into another food is a sign of opulence. Similarly, the third and fourth questions. We eat *karpas* dipped in salt water, which is reminiscent of Jewish pain and tears, yet we recline as a show of redemption. In essence, the Four Questions touch upon the paradox of Seder night, when the symbols of servitude and suffering intertwine with those of redemption.

THE FOUR QUESTIONS

Why is this night different from all other nights?

מַה נִּשְׁתַּנָּה הַלַּיְלָה הַזֶּה מִכָּל הַלֵּילוֹת?

1) On all other nights we eat either leavened bread or unleavened (matzah); on this night why only unleavened bread?

שֶׁבְּכָל הַלֵּילוֹת אָנוּ אוֹכְלִין חָמֵץ וּמַצָּה, הַלַּיְלָה הַזֶּה כֻּלּוֹ מַצָּה:

2) On all other nights we eat herbs of any kind; on this night why only bitter herbs?

שֶׁבְּכָל הַלֵּילוֹת אָנוּ אוֹכְלִין שְׁאָר יְרָקוֹת, הַלַּיְלָה הַזֶּה (כֻּלּוֹ) מָרוֹר:

3) On all other nights we do not dip our herbs even once; on this night why do we dip them twice?

שֶׁבְּכָל הַלֵּילוֹת אֵין אָנוּ מַטְבִּילִין, אֲפִילוּ פַּעַם אֶחָת, הַלַּיְלָה הַזֶּה שְׁתֵּי פְעָמִים:

4) On all other nights we eat our meals in any manner; on this night why do we sit around the table together in a reclining position?

שֶׁבְּכָל הַלֵּילוֹת אָנוּ אוֹכְלִין, בֵּין יוֹשְׁבִין, וּבֵין מְסֻבִּין, הַלַּיְלָה הַזֶּה כֻּלָּנוּ מְסֻבִּין:

The fundamental questions have been asked, and in *maggid* we shall find the answers. Of course, it is the duty of the older generation (not only the father) to respond to the questions and relate them to the Seder and all that it stands for. Ironically, in our own time, with the growth of the *baal teshuvah* movement, when many children have become far more committed to Jewish tradition than their parents and much more knowledgeable, the Seder night might be the occasion for the younger generation to answer the questions posed by the parents and grandparents.

AVADIM HAYYINU   עֲבָדִים הָיִינוּ לְפַרְעֹה

The Talmud declares that "we begin with the shame and conclude with the praise" (*Pesaḥim* 116a). This is the principle that governs the order we follow in *maggid*. However, the Sages disagree on what "the shame" refers to. Rav maintains "the shame" is that "originally our fathers were idolaters." Shmuel counters with "we were slaves in Egypt." This difference of opinion goes to the heart of our celebration on Passover night.

Rav says that our fathers were idolaters, and on Passover we celebrate our liberation from idolatry. The real shame in Egypt was not the physical servitude but the spiritual enslavement. The Jews were so strongly influenced by the idolatrous practices of the Egyptians that they did not truly believe in their God. The triumph then celebrates our being set free to become worshippers of the Almighty God. Shmuel holds, however, that the real shame is the physical enslavement and the denigration of the human personality, and what we thus celebrate is our physical emancipation. The Haggadah combines both opinions, therefore imparting the lesson that our shame was both the physical as well as the spiritual enslavement and that in the end we rejoice over our physical freedom as well as our newfound nearness to the Almighty. We begin the Haggadah, nevertheless, with the position of Shmuel: "We were slaves unto Pharaoh in Egypt."

Uncover the matzah and begin the reply.

THE ANSWER

We were slaves of Pharaoh in Egypt, and the Eternal our God brought us out from there with a strong hand and an outstretched arm. Now if God had not brought out our forefathers from Egypt, then even we, our children, and our children's children might still have been enslaved to Pharaoh in Egypt. Therefore, even were we all wise, all men of understanding, and even if we were all sages and well learned in the Torah, it would still be our duty to tell the story of the departure from Egypt. And the more one elaborates upon the story of the departure from Egypt, the more he is to be praised.

עֲבָדִים הָיִינוּ לְפַרְעֹה בְּמִצְרָיִם, וַיּוֹצִיאֵנוּ יְיָ אֱלֹהֵינוּ מִשָּׁם, בְּיָד חֲזָקָה וּבִזְרֹעַ נְטוּיָה, וְאִלּוּ לֹא הוֹצִיא הַקָּדוֹשׁ בָּרוּךְ הוּא, אֶת־ אֲבוֹתֵינוּ מִמִּצְרַיִם, הֲרֵי אָנוּ, וּבָנֵינוּ וּבְנֵי בָנֵינוּ, מְשֻׁעְבָּדִים הָיִינוּ לְפַרְעֹה בְּמִצְרָיִם, וַאֲפִילוּ כֻּלָּנוּ חֲכָמִים, כֻּלָּנוּ נְבוֹנִים, כֻּלָּנוּ זְקֵנִים, כֻּלָּנוּ יוֹדְעִים אֶת־הַתּוֹרָה, מִצְוָה עָלֵינוּ לְסַפֵּר בִּיצִיאַת מִצְרָיִם. וְכָל־הַמַּרְבֶּה לְסַפֵּר בִּיצִיאַת מִצְרַיִם הֲרֵי זֶה מְשֻׁבָּח:

The Story of the Five Sages

The story of the five sages in Bene-Berak is more intriguing than it is revealing. Several points are worthy of note. The five rabbis were certainly well versed in the story of the Exodus; yet they continued to speak of it all night long. It is also strange that their students had to come in to remind the rabbis to recite the morning *Shema*. Didn't the rabbis remember? Were they so engrossed in the story that they had lost track of time? Is it not arrogant of the students to remind their rabbis? There is a current joke in Israel that this behavior is typical of Bene-Berak, where the students inform their teachers about proper religious conduct. In any case there must be more to the story than what meets the eye.

Several suggestions have been made, among which the most popular is that the rabbis sitting all night in Bene-Berak were planning the overthrow of the Roman government. In the morning their students arrived to tell them that the morning star had arisen (i.e., it was day—a symbol of freedom) and that it was time to carry out the revolt and declare loyalty to the One God only. But this explanation is historically unlikely. Perhaps, therefore, a slightly different, allegorical interpretation is in order—one which also takes into account the following passage in the Haggadah concerning the controversy between Ben Zoma and the Rabbis.

These disputants argued over the obligation to mention the Exodus in the evening *Shema*. Figuratively, their disagreement goes much deeper. Night is generally a symbol of darkness and servitude. Day is a symbol of freedom and redemption. Yet the Passover Seder begins at night because we believe that the Almighty will redeem us in the darkness of the night. "The salvation of the Lord arrives in the blink of an eye." Ben Zoma felt that one should always remember the going out of Egypt—even at night—for we may never cease hoping for redemption. In the darkest exile, during the most violent persecution, even during the long night of the Roman tyranny, we can never lose faith in God our Redeemer. But the Sages disagreed. They believed that hope and faith are not sufficient. It is not enough simply to recite the *Shema* and remind ourselves of the Exodus from Egypt. To bring about the final redemption and the exodus from *galut* requires more than prayer and study—it requires activism. This is the meaning of לְהָבִיא לִימוֹת הַמָּשִׁיחַ. Put in other terms, the issue revolved around וְחַי בָּהֶם ("And *live* by them") vs. וְהִתְגַּדִּלְתִּי וְהִתְקַדִּשְׁתִּי ("And I shall be glorified and sanctified"). Were the Jews to be satisfied with the fact that the Roman government tolerated them and allowed them to exist, or were they to strive for a political and religious independence that would be the glory of God? Ben Zoma counseled against risking the former, but the Rabbis insisted on the latter.

This very question of activism vs. pacifism was the issue that was debated by the sages in Bene-Berak. R. Akiba, as is well known, was a champion of Bar Kokhba and adopted a militaristic approach against the Roman Empire. His colleagues were generally opposed to open hostilities and preached a peaceful coexistence with the vast empire. This debate raged all night—in the context of the Passover Seder and the redemption from Egypt. But in the morning the disciples, in their zeal for independence from Rome, insisted that the Jews must act—even fight—to bring about their freedom. The morning star had arisen; it was time to recite the *Shema* and to confirm the kingship of God. The Roman yoke had to be removed and a new independent Jewish commonwealth established.

Tragically R. Akiba and his disciples failed, and Bar Kokhba proved not to be the Messiah. Perhaps the Jews were not yet ready; perhaps it was that the students of R. Akiba, as the Talmud teaches, did not have sufficient respect for one another (Jerusalem was destroyed because of careless hatred) and we were not yet morally worthy of the Messiah. After Bar Kokhba's defeat the Jews realized that they could do no more than hold on to וָחַי בָּהֶם, living in accord with divine law despite *galut* and persecution. The time for true independence had to wait for the distant future.

And so for two thousand years the Jews only dreamed and prayed for the Holy Land. But all that changed with the Holocaust. After the experience of Auschwitz and Treblinka the Jews realized that without the וְהִתְגַּדִּלְתִּי וְהִתְקַדִּשְׁתִּי there can be no וָחַי בָּהֶם. Without their own independent state there can be no surety of their existence. For R. Akiba it was too early for redemption, but for us in the post-Holocaust period, the Messianic era cannot be too far off.

It is told that Rabbi Eliezer, Rabbi Joshua, Rabbi Elazar the son of Azariah, Rabbi Akiba and Rabbi Tarfon sat all night in Bene-Berak telling the story

מַעֲשֶׂה בְּרַבִּי אֱלִיעֶזֶר, וְרַבִּי יְהוֹשֻׁעַ, וְרַבִּי אֶלְעָזָר בֶּן־עֲזַרְיָה, וְרַבִּי עֲקִיבָא, וְרַבִּי טַרְפוֹן, שֶׁהָיוּ מְסֻבִּין בִּבְנֵי־בְרַק, וְהָיוּ מְסַפְּרִים

of the departure from Egypt. Towards morning their students came to tell them that it was time for the recitation of the morning Shema.

בִּיצִיאַת מִצְרַיִם, כָּל־אוֹתוֹ הַלַּיְלָה, עַד שֶׁבָּאוּ תַלְמִידֵיהֶם וְאָמְרוּ לָהֶם: רַבּוֹתֵינוּ, הִגִּיעַ זְמַן קְרִיאַת־שְׁמַע, שֶׁל שַׁחֲרִית:

Rabbi Elazar the son of Azariah said: Here I am a man of seventy years, yet I did not understand why the story of the departure from Egypt should be told at night, until Ben Zoma explained it. The Bible commands us, saying: "That you may remember the day of your going out from Egypt all the days of your life." Ben Zoma explained: The *days of your life* might mean only the days: *all the days of your life*

אָמַר רַבִּי אֶלְעָזָר בֶּן־עֲזַרְיָה. הֲרֵי אֲנִי כְּבֶן שִׁבְעִים שָׁנָה, וְלֹא זָכִיתִי, שֶׁתֵּאָמֵר יְצִיאַת מִצְרַיִם בַּלֵּילוֹת, עַד שֶׁדְּרָשָׁהּ בֶּן זוֹמָא. שֶׁנֶּאֱמַר: לְמַעַן תִּזְכֹּר, אֶת־יוֹם צֵאתְךָ מֵאֶרֶץ מִצְרַיִם, כֹּל יְמֵי חַיֶּיךָ. יְמֵי חַיֶּיךָ הַיָּמִים, כֹּל יְמֵי חַיֶּיךָ הַלֵּילוֹת. וַחֲכָמִים אוֹמְרִים: יְמֵי חַיֶּיךָ הָעוֹלָם הַזֶּה. כֹּל יְמֵי חַיֶּיךָ לְהָבִיא לִימוֹת הַמָּשִׁיחַ:

includes the nights as well. The other sages, however, explain it this way: The *days of your life* refers to this world only, but *all the days of your life* includes also the time of the Messiah.

BARUCH HA-MAKOM

בָּרוּךְ הַמָּקוֹם

What are we actually doing when we read the Haggadah? We are learning Torah.

The Seder meal is a meal par excellence because it is the occasion for Torah study. *Maggid* allows for each parent to become a *rebbe*, each child a *talmid*, and each dining room table a miniature study house.

The passage beginning with בָּרוּךְ הַמָּקוֹם (lit. "blessed be the Place") is actually a kind of blessing, as Rabbi Soloveitchik has explained. Of course, technically there is no need to recite a blessing over the Torah at this time since the morning blessings are sufficient to cover Torah study throughout the day until the next morning. Nevertheless, because of the special occasion, a special blessing was introduced—albeit without the mention of God's Name.

We refer to God as the *Makom*, or "Place of the World," to indicate that the whole universe is His place. There is no place which is devoid of his presence. Jews reject pantheism, according to which everything is God, but they are comfortable with panentheism, a Greek term denoting that everything is in God, i.e., encompassed by God. On Passover it is particularly appropriate to use הַמָּקוֹם in reference to the Almighty since this holiday celebrates God's role in history. Only an imminent God who is in—but not limited by—this world could have redeemed the Jews and led them out of Egypt.

On a more metaphoric level, we also recite "Blessed be the Place" because we are blessing the place around which everyone is seated at the Seder—the place of family togetherness, the place of Divine celebration over the meal, the place of Torah study. Blessed and praised be this place, and blessed be the One who gave Torah to His people Israel, the Torah that taught us to establish such a place on the night of the fifteenth of Nisan.

Blessed is God, Who gave the Torah to His people Israel. Blessed is He. The Torah speaks about four children: one who is wise and one who is wicked; one who is simple and one who does not even know how to ask a question.	בָּרוּךְ הַמָּקוֹם. בָּרוּךְ הוּא. בָּרוּךְ שֶׁנָּתַן תּוֹרָה לְעַמּוֹ יִשְׂרָאֵל. בָּרוּךְ הוּא. כְּנֶגֶד אַרְבָּעָה בָנִים דִּבְּרָה תוֹרָה. אֶחָד חָכָם, וְאֶחָד רָשָׁע, וְאֶחָד תָּם, וְאֶחָד שֶׁאֵינוֹ יוֹדֵעַ לִשְׁאוֹל:

Now that we have pronounced the blessing we can begin to learn Torah. We turn to the passage dealing with the Four Children, which is really a Passover midrash based on several verses in the Torah.

The Four Children*

There are (at least) four different types of children who will grow into different types of adults. The parent who is to teach effectively must fit the manner of study to the quality and capacity for understanding of each of his children. Education cannot be mass-produced, for each child (and adult) is a world unto himself, and the parent/teacher must be sensitive to each world. Similarly, a rabbi who has a single, inflexible approach in teaching Torah to his congregation is making a serious error. It is imperative to have different answers for each questioner and to relate them not only to the substance of the question but also to the personality of the questioner. Thus, the Haggadah speaks of four children to indicate that each one is to be taught and instructed in a manner suitable for him or her.

The Wise Child

The Wise Child asks, "What are the testimonies, the statutes, and the judgments that the Lord our God has commanded you?" From this question one can perceive a searching, intellectual spirit. He divides the laws of the Torah into three categories. The *edot* ("testimonies") are laws that bear witness to the existence of the people of God. These are laws that unite us as a nation, such as ritual laws. The *ḥukkim* are statutes for which there are no discernible reasons. We observe them even though we do not necessarily understand them because they link us to the Divine. Rav Saadia Gaon suggests that as civilization progresses, more and more of these laws will be understood, because our Torah is indeed the quintessence of Divine wisdom. We observe *ḥukkim* because as Jews we believe that they were commanded by a God who loves us and is concerned for our well-being. And finally the *mishpatim* ("judgments") are rational, ethical laws which every intelligent person

---

° בָּנִים in this context refers to both sons and daughters.

can well understand. Put in slightly different words, the *hukkim* link us to God, the *edot* to our people, and the *mishpatim* to society.

The parent-teacher must explain all of these laws to the Wise Child, up to and including the law dealing with the *afikoman* (אֵין מַפְטִירִין אַחַר הַפֶּסַח אֲפִיקוֹמָן), which is the subject of the last mishnah in *Pesahim* that deals with the Seder night. Hence you are to teach the wise child all of the laws of Passover from beginning to end, from the proper preparation of the festival to the conclusion of the Seder night with its final prohibition.

Another reason for mentioning the particular law of the *afikoman* to the Wise Child is that this passage of the Mishnah has an interesting metaphoric interpretation. On a halakhic level it prohibits eating anything substantial after the paschal sacrifice or after the final piece of matzah, whose taste must remain in the celebrant's mouth. But eating can also symbolize the physical. The Wise Child has asked several intelligent questions. His approach to life is intellectual. He wants to understand and to reason, and you must instruct him. However, you must also teach him that Judaism is not merely an intellectual pursuit. While he may comprehend the laws cognitively, he should also remember the taste of the matzah. It is not enough only to study Judaism; one must also practice it. And the joy of practicing should be as a pleasant taste on the tongue remaining long after the actual performance of the mitzvah.

The wise child asks: "What is the meaning of the testimonies, statutes, and judgments which the Eternal our God has commanded us?" You shall explain to him all the laws of Passover, to the very last detail about the *afikoman*.

חָכָם מָה הוּא אוֹמֵר. מָה הָעֵדֹת וְהַחֻקִּים וְהַמִּשְׁפָּטִים, אֲשֶׁר צִוָּה יְיָ אֱלֹהֵינוּ אֶתְכֶם? וְאַף אַתָּה אֱמָר־ לוֹ כְּהִלְכוֹת הַפֶּסַח: אֵין מַפְטִירִין אַחַר הַפֶּסַח אֲפִיקוֹמָן:

The Wicked Child

What does the Wicked Child say? "What is this service to *you*? To you and not to himself. Because he excludes himself from the peoplehood of Israel, he denies the basic principle of our faith." Thus can we translate the Hebrew, although there are different renderings as well. According to our translation, the Haggadah defines a *koffar ba-ikkar*—one who denies the basic principle of our faith—as he who disassociates himself from the Jewish people. The unity of the Jewish people is the first principle of our religion. The Wicked Child denies this not by transgressing a specific command- ment but by verbally transforming the "us" to a "you." Refusing to include himself in *kelal yisrael* consigns him to the worst of appro- bations—a *koffar ba-ikkar*.

How are we to respond to the Wicked Child? The Haggadah suggests that we "set his teeth on edge." This means that we do not really answer the substance of his question, which in essence has already been answered with *avadim hayyinu*. Instead we answer him in his own terms. ". . . because God took *me* out of the Land of Egypt, me and not you." We tell him in effect that on this night every Jew must reexperience Jewish history, and "you, *rasha*, who are excluding yourself from such a reexperience, should know that had you lived at that time, you would not have been redeemed." Indeed, the Jews who disassociated themselves at that time from the destiny of their people remained in Egypt and disappeared among the anonymous slave population (according to the Midrash).

From another perspective, one can ask if the Wicked Child is truly wicked. After all, he has joined his family at their Seder, though his views are quite radical and even heretical. Perhaps we can best disarm him by including him in the Seder, by warming him with Seder wine and imparting to him the "Torah" of the Seder. It should be noted, in fact, that the most problematic child is not the *rasha*, the so-called Wicked Child, but rather the one who does not even show up at the Seder.

The commentaries ask the obvious question. If the Wicked Child excludes himself, is it not also true that the Wise Child excludes himself? The *rasha* says, "What is this service to *you*," but the *hakham* also says, "What are these testimonies, statutes, and judgments which the Lord has commanded *you*." Both speak in terms of "you"; both distance themselves. Actually, though, the difference is very clear. First, the Wise Child includes himself by mentioning *Hashem Elokeinu*—the Lord *our* God. Not only does he mention God, which the Wicked Child does not, but he uses the pronoun "our." Second, he uses the term אֶתְכֶם, which does not imply self-exclusion, in contradistinction to the *rasha*'s לָכֶם ("to you"). The third and most crucial difference between the two children lies not so much in what they say but in how they say it. The Wise Child addresses himself to content, asking detailed questions; the Wicked Child challenges the whole ritual, lumping everything into *avodah*. The *rasha* sets up a negative relationship between himself and his family. The *hakham*, on the other hand, inquires into the rituals which tie family and nation together. He asks about the "within." The Wicked Child stops short at the "without."

The questions of both children emanate from the Bible. The query of the Wicked Child comes from Exodus 12:26: "And it shall be when your children *say* unto you, 'What is this service of yours?'" The Wise Child's question is found in Deuteronomy 6:20: "When your child will *ask* you tomorrow, saying, 'What are the testimonies, the statutes, and the judgments which the Lord our God has commanded you?'" Note that the Wicked Child "says" and the Wise Child "asks." When the younger generation begin their search not by questioning but by dictating, by "telling," then they are in trouble. While there can be ultimate disagreement, the beginning of the search must be conducted out of a spirit of questioning, out of honest, sincere, humble awareness of one's unknowingness.

A young child once asked his father, "Why is it that when you wheel baby brother in his carriage you look so happy. But when you push Grandpa in his wheelchair you look as if you were about to cry?" The father responded: "When a father leads his child, the father smiles and the child smiles. When a child must lead his father, the child cries and the father cries." The secret of our tradition is the child's willingness to follow the parents by asking about the heritage that they are transmitting.

And finally it should be noted that the Torah states, in connection with the Wise Child, "When your child will ask you *tomorrow*. . . ." This indicates that the *hakham* performs first and then asks. The Wicked Child, on the other hand, questions first as a condition for his performance and uses aggressive language as an excuse for his nonperformance. The Wise Child responds as the Jewish people did at Mount Sinai: נַעֲשֶׂה וְנִשְׁמָע (Ex. 24:7)—"we shall do and then we shall [attempt to] understand." *Mahar* ("tomorrow") indicates that the Wise Child attended a Seder and performed the mitzvot. Now he seeks to know why. Judaism insists that the performance of a commandment must precede questions about it, although full freedom is given to ask after its observance. This is the essential difference between a people of revelation, such as the Jewish people, and a people of reason, such as the Greeks. Judaism believes that the understanding of the act is derived from its performance. One cannot analyze a Divine commandment in the abstract without first having observed it in deed. One must appropriate the commandment and make it one's own; then one may speak about it or question it from within. This does not imply the absolutism of dogma; it reflects the simple logic that one cannot reject out of hand what one has not yet experienced. It is also the modern, "existentialist" position of Franz Rosenzweig. If you want to reject the Sabbath, first experience it with sensitivity and participation. As Rosenzweig's own life attests, once one has truly experienced a Jewish ritual, one no longer wishes to cast it off.

The wicked child asks: "What is the meaning of this service to you!" Saying *you*, he excludes himself, and because he excludes himself from the group, he denies a basic principle of our faith. You in turn should set his teeth on edge and say to him: "Because of what the Eternal did for me when I came forth from Egypt" I do this. For *me* and not for *him*; had he been there, he would not have been redeemed.

רָשָׁע מָה הוּא אוֹמֵר. מָה הָעֲבֹדָה הַזֹּאת לָכֶם! לָכֶם וְלֹא לוֹ. וּלְפִי שֶׁהוֹצִיא אֶת־עַצְמוֹ מִן הַכְּלָל, כָּפַר בָּעִקָּר. וְאַף אַתָּה הַקְהֵה אֶת־שִׁנָּיו, וֶאֱמָר־לוֹ: בַּעֲבוּר זֶה, עָשָׂה יְיָ לִי, בְּצֵאתִי מִמִּצְרָיִם. לִי וְלֹא־לוֹ. אִלּוּ הָיָה שָׁם, לֹא הָיָה נִגְאָל:

The Simple Child

The *tam* asks, "What is this?" His question is simple and your response must be simple. "With a strong hand God took us out of Egypt, from the house of slavery." We usually think of the *tam* as a simpleton, and we associate the brevity of his question with simple-mindedness. This, however, may not be a correct interpretation. In the Bible, *tam* is a term of praise, as it is written: "You shall be wholehearted (*tam*) with the Lord your God" (Deut. 18:13). *Tam* connotes honesty and forthrightness. Our father Jacob was described as an אִישׁ תָּם, who dwelt in the tents of Torah (Gen. 25:27). He was complete in the sense that his exterior reflected his interior—no deceit and no disingenousness.

A great Hasidic teacher, Reb Nachman of Bratslav, insisted that he spent all of his life attempting with every fiber of his mind to achieve *temimut* (from the root *tam*)—religious naivete and whole-heartedness. In the deepest sense of the word, *tam* represents in the writings of the mystics the very highest level of religious consciousness. It represents the sincerity and eagerness to do God's will as well as to truly love and serve one's fellow man.

Accordingly, the *tam*, the so-called Simple Child, should be viewed in a different light. He is not the opposite of the Wise Child intellectually, but rather the opposite of the Wicked Child religiously. We can thus divide the Four Children into two groups each with its own contrasting pair. In one group the children differ in their intellectual abilities: the Wise Child vs. the Child Who Does Not Know How To Ask. In the second group the spiritual differences between two children are highlighted; one is the *tam*, or the Religiously Naive Child, while his opposite is the Wicked Child.

The simple child asks: "What is this?" To him you shall say: "With a strong hand the Eternal brought us out of Egypt, from the house of bondage."	תָּם מָה הוּא אוֹמֵר. מַה זֹּאת? וְאָמַרְתָּ אֵלָיו: בְּחֹזֶק יָד הוֹצִיאָנוּ יְיָ מִמִּצְרַיִם מִבֵּית עֲבָדִים:

The Child Who Does Not Know How to Ask

The last of the Four Children is the one who does not know what to ask or even that he is supposed to ask. The Haggadah begins: אַתְּ פְּתַח לוֹ—you must begin for him. אַתְּ, as the commentators have noticed, is in the feminine gender to suggest that our approach to this child should be "feminine"—with understanding, love, and sweetness, with the warmth prototypically associated with the mother. Anticipate and bring out his questions slowly, and give him answers he can understand. Also, אַתְּ begins with the first letter of the Hebrew alphabet and ends with the last to indicate, as the commentaries suggest, that we are to teach him from *aleph* to *tav*, the alpha and omega of Jewish life—with love and sensitivity.

In our generation we are overwhelmingly faced with those who do not know how to ask. It is not the problem of those who reject, but those who do not know. אַתְּ פְּתַח לוֹ becomes the obligation of the older generation—to prompt one's questions, to make it so that he or she will begin to ask. If they do not ask, then all of our answers will be in vain. There is no point in answering before the question has been asked. Rav Levi Yitzhak of Berditchev would often characterize himself as the "son who does not even know what to ask," and he prayed at each Seder that the Almighty would "open up" to him and reveal the proper questions.

As for the child who does not even know how to ask a question, you must begin for him, as it is written in the Bible: "You shall tell your child on that day: This is done because of that which the Eternal did for me when I came forth out of Egypt."

וְשֶׁאֵינוֹ יוֹדֵעַ לִשְׁאוֹל, אַתְּ פְּתַח לוֹ. שֶׁנֶּאֱמַר: וְהִגַּדְתָּ לְבִנְךָ, בַּיּוֹם הַהוּא לֵאמֹר: בַּעֲבוּר זֶה עָשָׂה יְיָ לִי, בְּצֵאתִי מִמִּצְרָיִם:

Four Children, Four Generations

According to a delightful interpretation ascribed to the former Lubavitcher Rebbe, Rabbi Joseph Isaac Schneersohn (1880–1950), the Four Children represent the four generations of the American experience. The Wise Child represents the European roots, the generation of the grandparents who came to America with beard and earlocks, dressed in *streimel* and *kapote*, steeped in piety, with a love for learning and profound knowledge of the Jewish tradition.

Their progeny (the Wicked Child), brought up within the American "melting pot," rejected his parent's customs and ways of thought. He thought of himself as being in a new country with new ways of thinking and acting. To him, the parents were terribly old-fashioned and a bit foolish for not immediately adopting the new ways, which seemed more easygoing and profitable. Turning his back on the glories of the Jewish tradition, this child often became successful in business but was cynical in his outlook.

The third generation, the Simple Child is confused. He watched his grandfather making *Kiddush* on Friday night and his father standing by silently, perhaps resentfully, impatient to prepare for business on Saturday morning. The memory of this grandfather, though strong at one time, is fading, and so the confused Simple Child can only ask "מַה זֹּאת," caught as he is in the conflict between his grandfather and his father.

The fourth generation, the Child Who Does Not Know How to Ask, offspring of the Simple Child, is the greatest tragedy of all. He was born after his great-grandparents had died. He knows only his totally assimilated grandfather, the *rasha*, and his religiously confused father. He does not even know how to ask questions. This is our mute American generation, the generation of the child who thought it was someone's birthday when she saw her great-grandmother lighting the festival candles. The only time this child had seen candles being lit was on birthdays. She did not even know how to ask. We are now being challenged to open our great heritage to this generation which lost it without ever knowing what it had possessed.°

There is also a fifth generation, which is merely hinted at in the Haggadah. This generation is so far removed from Judaism that it does not even know it is Passover. No matter what we say about the Wicked Child, at least he is at the Seder. The One Who Does Not Know How to Ask somehow stumbled upon a Seder even if he finds it rather incomprehensible. But that fifth generation, which is rapidly becoming the dominant Jewish generation in America, is not here at all. When we open the door for Elijah the prophet, we must hold the door open for every Jew who has not yet come in. And then perhaps not only the fifth generation but the prophet

---

° I was actually at a Seder where a child began singing "Happy Birthday" when she saw her great-grandmother lighting candles in honor of the Passover festival.

Elijah too will come in "to restore the hearts of the children to the parents and the hearts of the parents to the children" (Mal. 3:24). And only when the door is held wide open, only when we learn to speak to those fifth-generation children, only when we restore all of them to their lost heritage, shall we be privileged to usher in complete redemption.

יָכוֹל מֵרֹאשׁ חֹדֶשׁ

After giving us examples of four children and four respective approaches to their instruction, the Haggadah continues to teach us how to effectively impart the story and the meaning of the Exodus. "One would think that we ought to begin our celebration on Rosh Ḥodesh." Why at the beginning of the month? Because the whole month became associated with redemption. The Israelites began to prepare for their departure days before the fifteenth of Nisan. The beginning of the month would have been a logical point at which to begin, especially since the mitzvah to sanctify Rosh Ḥodesh was actually the first commandment given to the Jewish people as a nation ("This month shall be to you the first month of the year"— Ex. 12:2). Nevertheless, the Haggadah tells us that we begin our celebration on the fifteenth of Nisan, the day that we actually left Egypt.

"If on the fifteenth, one might think that we start during the day." This suggestion is also rejected in favor of starting—as is derived from the Torah—at night. We are bidden to celebrate Passover when the physical objects associated with the holiday, namely, the matzah and *maror,* are before us—on Passover eve. The lesson that we can derive is that the Torah in general, and the Exodus story in particular, should not be taught in a dry, scholastic manner. Not only our minds but also our senses should take part in learning. We need the physical, ritual object to stimulate our minds and to attract us emotionally to the mitzvah. The cognitive process alone is insufficient; it must be accompanied by concrete "visual aids." On Passover these are the matzah and *maror.* Since these must be eaten on the fifteenth at night, our celebration too takes place at night. We might have here at the Seder the very first example of teaching with visual aids in the history of education.

One might think that the Seder ceremony should be performed on the first day of Nisan. The Torah therefore tells us "on that day"—on Passover. Saying "on that day," one might suppose that the Seder should be conducted during the daytime.

יָכוֹל מֵרֹאשׁ חֹדֶשׁ, תַּלְמוּד לוֹמַר בַּיּוֹם הַהוּא. אִי בַּיּוֹם הַהוּא, יָכוֹל מִבְּעוֹד יוֹם. תַּלְמוּד לוֹמַר, בַּעֲבוּר זֶה. בַּעֲבוּר זֶה לֹא אָמַרְתִּי, אֶלָּא בְּשָׁעָה שֶׁיֵּשׁ מַצָּה וּמָרוֹר, מֻנָּחִים לְפָנֶיךָ:

But inasmuch as the Torah adds "because of *this*," I learn from it that the ceremony does not begin until the time when unleavened bread (matzah) and bitter herbs are set before you—on Passover night.

מִתְּחִלָּה עוֹבְדֵי עֲבוֹדָה זָרָה הָיוּ אֲבוֹתֵינוּ

We have concluded the first part of *maggid* with the mention of our physical enslavement and subsequent freedom—in accordance with the view of Shmuel. We are now ready to begin the second part, where we refer to our original spiritual degradation and ultimate redemption, which is what Rav considered the essence of the Haggadah. °

There is an important distinction between Rav's Haggadah and that of Shmuel about which we have not yet spoken, namely, how to interpret the present condition of the Jews in light of the notion of יְצִיאַת מִצְרַיִם. How can we say that we (through our ancestors) were slaves in Egypt and *then we became free* when there are still millions of Jews, behind the Iron Curtain and elsewhere, for whom these words are but a dream? Indeed Rav can respond that "free" is to be understood in a spiritual sense and that Jews, shackled as they may be, are spiritually free because they received the Torah. But Shmuel's reading, which emphasizes the physical and political aspect of freedom, certainly requires explanation in view of current, as well as past, experience.

To this problem we might respond that the recitation of the

° See our discussion of Rav and Shmuel above.

Haggadah represents an act of faith for the future as much as an affirmation of the past. The Exodus from Egypt is not just an important historical event; it is a prototype of God's relationship to His people. As He took them/us out of the bondage of Egypt, so will He free the Jews from the Russian labor camps, the Iranian prisons, etc. Because of our experience in Egypt, we trust in God as our Redeemer. There will be other Exoduses from other Egypts. Thus we can say—despite the wretched conditions that many Jews find themselves in today—that we became free.

There is a story about a Jew who returned from shul one Sabbath to find his house completely destroyed and his family scattered by the marauding Cossacks. It was *Shabbat Ha-Gadol*, the Sabbath before Passover, one of the two Sabbaths of the year on which the rabbi is traditionally obligated to hold a lengthy discourse. Though heartbroken and bereft of food and shelter, the Jew went to hear Rabbi Joshua Heschel, the Apter Rebbe. In the midst of the ruin wrought by the Cossacks, the rebbe spoke of Passover as a time of redemption. The unfortunate Jew returned to his wrecked home, to the desolate remains of what had once been his, and at the conclusion of the Sabbath could be seen dancing among the ruins and singing the praises of God.

The key to the survival of our people is in the belief that regardless of our physical plight, we are redeemed religiously and spiritually. Seen from this perspective, the celebration of Passover is a personal and immediate experience. מִצְרַיִם, the Hebrew word for "Egypt," is explained by the Zohar as derived from מְצָרִים, which means "narrow straits." Every Jew frequently finds himself in agonizing straits, sometimes for physical reasons, such as poverty, illness, tragic death, etc., and sometimes for psychological reasons, such as alienation, frustration, or despair. Passover teaches that the Almighty takes us out of these מְצָרִים. It is thus the holiday of hope and faith par excellence.

Along the lines of this interpretation, the mystics understood the Exodus from מצרים as the redemption from sin. Passover was completely removed from the historical and placed within the metaphysical plane affecting each and every Jew. The *galut* from which we seek redemption is not so much a physical concept, according to the mystics, as a spiritual category. They cite the story of Cain as proof. After he slew his brother, God meted out a special punishment for him. "A roamer and a wanderer shall you be in the land" (Gen. 4:12). This is followed by: "And Cain went out before the presence of God and dwelt in the land of Nod" (Gen. 4:16). How could Cain be a restless wanderer and at the same time dwell in the land of Nod? The apparent explanation is that once an individual leaves the presence of God, he feels himself alienated from the Divine and thinks of himself as living in a world in which there is no Divine protection. Given such a mentality, no matter where he has settled, he is "a wanderer and a roamer." He is in a state of spiritual wandering. He is cut off from his Divine root.

Jews are known as a wandering people. As the old Yiddish joke has it: Why do Jews wear hats? Because they are always ready to leave. But despite this categorization, most Jews never felt displaced, for wherever they went, they remained rooted in their God and in their history and tradition. On the other hand, there are wealthy American Jews who are spiritual wanderers even though they have never moved from this country—because they have lost their sense of Divine protection. On Passover this point is a major theme of the Haggadah: "Initially our forefathers were idolaters"—they were lost and uprooted. "But now the Almighty has brought us near to Him [literally, 'to His service']." Spiritually, we have been redeemed.

Long, ago our forefathers were worshippers of idols. Now the Eternal is our God and we worship Him. Even as the Bible tells us: "And Joshua said to all the people: Thus said the Eternal God of Israel: In days of old your forefathers lived beyond the river; that is, Terah, the father of Abraham and Nahor. They worshipped other gods. Then I took Abraham, your father, from beyond the river. I led him through the whole land

מִתְּחִלָּה עוֹבְדֵי עֲבוֹדָה זָרָה הָיוּ אֲבוֹתֵינוּ. וְעַכְשָׁו קֵרְבָנוּ הַמָּקוֹם לַעֲבוֹדָתוֹ. שֶׁנֶּאֱמַר: וַיֹּאמֶר יְהוֹשֻׁעַ אֶל־כָּל־הָעָם. כֹּה אָמַר יְיָ אֱלֹהֵי יִשְׂרָאֵל, בְּעֵבֶר הַנָּהָר יָשְׁבוּ אֲבוֹתֵיכֶם מֵעוֹלָם, תֶּרַח אֲבִי אַבְרָהָם וַאֲבִי נָחוֹר, וַיַּעַבְדוּ אֱלֹהִים אֲחֵרִים: וָאֶקַּח אֶת־ אֲבִיכֶם אֶת־אַבְרָהָם מֵעֵבֶר הַנָּהָר, וָאוֹלֵךְ אוֹתוֹ בְּכָל־אֶרֶץ כְּנָעַן.

of Canaan. Then I increased his family by giving him a son, Isaac. And I gave Isaac two sons, Jacob and Esau. To Esau I gave Mount Seir as a possession, but Jacob and his sons went down to Egypt."

וָאַרְבֶּה אֶת־זַרְעוֹ, וָאֶתֶּן־לוֹ אֶת־יִצְחָק: וָאֶתֵּן לְיִצְחָק אֶת־יַעֲקֹב וְאֶת־עֵשָׂו. וָאֶתֵּן לְעֵשָׂו אֶת־הַר שֵׂעִיר, לָרֶשֶׁת אוֹתוֹ. וְיַעֲקֹב וּבָנָיו יָרְדוּ מִצְרָיִם:

כְּמָה שֶׁאָמַר לְאַבְרָהָם אָבִינוּ בִּבְרִית בֵּין הַבְּתָרִים

The בְּרִית בֵּין הַבְּתָרִים (literally, "Covenant between the Pieces") is a cornerstone of Jewish theology and gives meaning to all of Jewish history. Let us carefully analyze it and the events leading up to it. After the difficult battle between the four kings and the five kings (Gen. 14), Abraham emerges victorious and for the first time appears as a major historical figure and international leader. The Almighty then appears to Abraham in a vision and assures him that his reward shall be very great (Gen. 15:1). But Abraham is worried that he will have no offspring. Our forefather longed for a child who would be his heir. He was the founder of a new faith; he had received a prophetic vision that he wanted to hand on to the next and all subsequent generations. Abraham acutely feels the tragedy of seeing his life's work and his dream perishing with him. The Almighty responds with a promise that Abraham will indeed be a father and that his seed will be as numerous as the stars of heaven (Gen. 15:5). At the time of this Divine promise, Abraham and his wife, Sarah, were already well past the age of physical vigor. But Abraham believed in God's word, and this was accounted to him as an act of merit (Gen. 15:6). Abraham emerges from this encounter as a man of faith par excellence.

In the next verse, the Almighty extends His promise: "I am the Lord who took you out of Ur of the Chaldees to give you this land as an inheritance." But suddenly Abraham becomes a skeptic: "How will I know that I shall inherit it?" The Almighty then commands Abraham to take a number of animals and cut them in half, and in another vision, Abraham and the mysterious Presence of God together pass between the pieces, thus concluding a covenant in the manner customary among the people of Abraham's time. At the conclusion of the vision, God makes another promise to Abraham in which He informs him that his descendants will be slaves in a strange land but that they will be enriched and set free (Gen. 15:7–14).

The biblical commentators are perplexed that the same Abraham who so readily accepted the miracle of Sarah having a child, though she was past the age of childbearing, suddenly cannot believe that his descendants will inherit the Land of Israel. Why did Abraham the man of faith turn into Abraham the doubter?° Rabbi Moses Naḥmanides' (1194–1270) response to this question illuminates one of the fundamental concepts of Jewish theology. Before the בְּרִית בֵּין הַבְּתָרִים Abraham felt that he had a special relationship with God. He regarded that relationship as akin to a contract. In every contractual relationship there are two mutually obligated parties. If one party does not fulfill its obligations, the other is free from doing its part. When Abraham was assured a child, he was full of confidence in the "contract," for he knew he could live up to his part of the agreement, namely, to be a loyal and righteous servant of the Almighty. But when it came to the promise that his descendants would inherit the land, Abraham was no longer so confident. "How do I know that I will inherit it?" he asks, meaning, "How do I know that they will be worthy of the inheritance?" Abraham understood that if his children were not worthy, God would not carry out His part of the agreement.

Responding to Abraham's anxiety, God explains that His relationship to the Jewish people is not contractual but that it is covenantal—it involves a *berit*. A contract can remain in force for as long as the parties abide by it or it can be revoked entirely; a covenant by definition is irrevocable, and a covenant with the Almighty is both irrevocable and eternal. God stood as the guarantor that there would always be a faithful remnant, that although there might be times of separation, there would be ultimate reunion between the people and the land. God became the eternal guarantor of the eternal covenant. The Jewish people is the *am ha-berit*, the people of the covenant, and all of Jewish history is the practical expression of this eternal Divine-human encounter.

° The following interpretation was first pointed out to me and expanded upon by one of my most revered teachers and colleagues, Rav Moshe Besdin ז״ל.

In his farewell speech to his people, Moses recalls the stipulations of the covenant as he warns the Children of Israel not to turn away from the Almighty. In His displeasure with their wicked ways God will turn away from them. Persecution and pogrom will pursue them at every step, but in the end He will not fail them. Because the Jews themselves will never completely abandon the Lord, "He will not forget the covenant which He made under oath [with your fathers]" (Deut. 4:25–31). While near-total assimilation might occur in the Diaspora, the Jews will never completely assimilate. Their bond to God will ultimately prevail. This almost miraculous force is evident in our very day.

Consider the case of Leonid Riegerman, whose story is but one of the many inspiring tales of courageous Russian refuseniks standing up to be counted as Jews. Born in Moscow, Riegerman was raised as a communist and an atheist, never having entered a synagogue. One day he chanced upon an English translation of the Bible in a library. Thumbing through its pages he read the passage about Joseph's encounter with a mysterious stranger (Gen. 37:15–17). "What are you seeking?" the stranger asks, and Joseph replies, "I am seeking my brothers." Suddenly tears welled up in Riegerman's eyes and an inchoate yearning arose in his soul. "I too am seeking my brothers," he cried. Looking around the library and realizing that no one there was really his brother, he ran directly to the Great Synagogue on Arkhipova Street, joining a line of people waiting to buy matzah for Passover. Leonid Riegerman went on to become a religious Jew, a refusenik, and one of the great heroes of our generation. Leonid Riegerman found the Torah; he found the Almighty. In a real sense, however, the Torah and the Almighty found Leonid Riegerman, and so it is with many in our time.

The following tale is a magnificent commentary on the biblical covenant. Two Hasidim always visited their Rebbe on the festival of Sukkot, and each year, on the way, they stopped at the same inn. One year the innkeeper approached them humbly. "You know that I am not a Hasid or a disciple of your Rebbe," he said, "but I have a great favor to ask of you. My wife and I have been married for ten years, but unfortunately we have not been blessed with a child. Please ask the Rebbe to pray for us." The Hasidim agreed to do so, and the next morning the innkeeper's wife began parading around the neighborhood with an expensive baby carriage. When her friends gathered to wish her Mazel Tov, she explained that she was not yet with child but would soon be, because the Rebbe was going to pray for her. The two Hasidim were embarrassed, because they knew that prayers do not always bring the hoped-for result, but they said nothing and continued on their journey, faithfully performing their mission when they arrived at the Rebbe's court.

The following year, when the two Hasidim returned to the inn, the baby's circumcision was in progress. The innkeeper, of course, was quite grateful and treated them as guests of honor. Later on one of the Hasidim went in to see the Rebbe. "You didn't even know the innkeeper," he complained, "but I am your trusted disciple. Every year I visit you, just as my father always came to your father. Yet I have been married for twenty years and I don't have a child. Every year for the past twenty years, I've made the same request of you, and my wife still has not conceived. Rebbe, is it fair?" The Rebbe took his disciple's hands and looked deeply into his eyes. "During all those twenty years did you ever buy a baby carriage? How great was *your* faith compared to that of the innkeeper's wife?"

For the past two thousand years of life in the Diaspora, the Jews have always had the baby carriage ready. Despite oppression and discrimination, they never lost faith; they always believed that there will be ultimate redemption. In Auschwitz and Treblinka Jews went to the gas chambers with the words of *Shema Yisrael* and *Ani Ma'amin* on their lips. Their lives were crushed but not their souls, for they knew that their link with God would transcend their own wretched physical plight.

We have a Bible with the promise of a covenant, and that promise has sustained us through every generation. If you want to understand whence came the strength of a people driven from country to country; if you want to understand whence came the indomitable will of the Jews in the Soviet Union and now in America, where religious communities continue to flourish against all logic; if you want to understand whence came the spiritual strength of a people who were removed from the Land of Israel for more years than they ever lived in it and who cry out every year their hope לְשָׁנָה הַבָּאָה בִּירוּשָׁלָיִם; if you want to understand the powerful memory of a people that insists upon maintaining itself, never forgetting Israel but fighting and dying for it, you must look to the בְּרִית בֵּין הַבְּתָרִים, the beginning of whose fulfillment we are privileged to see in our lifetime.

Blessed be God, Who keeps His promise to Israel, blessed be He. For God foretold the end of the bondage to Abraham at the Covenant of the Pieces [Sacrifices]. For God said to Abraham: "Know that your children will be strangers in a land not their own. They will be enslaved there and will be oppressed for four hundred years. The nation who will oppress them shall, however, be judged. Afterward they will come forth with great wealth."

בָּרוּךְ שׁוֹמֵר הַבְטָחָתוֹ לְיִשְׂרָאֵל. בָּרוּךְ הוּא. שֶׁהַקָּדוֹשׁ בָּרוּךְ הוּא חִשֵּׁב אֶת־הַקֵּץ לַעֲשׂוֹת, כְּמָה שֶׁאָמַר לְאַבְרָהָם אָבִינוּ בִּבְרִית בֵּין הַבְּתָרִים. שֶׁנֶּאֱמַר: וַיֹּאמֶר לְאַבְרָם, יָדֹעַ תֵּדַע, כִּי־גֵר יִהְיֶה זַרְעֲךָ, בְּאֶרֶץ לֹא לָהֶם, וַעֲבָדוּם וְעִנּוּ אֹתָם. אַרְבַּע מֵאוֹת שָׁנָה: וְגַם אֶת־הַגּוֹי אֲשֶׁר יַעֲבֹדוּ, דָּן אָנֹכִי. וְאַחֲרֵי־כֵן יֵצְאוּ, בִּרְכֻשׁ גָּדוֹל:

וְהִיא שֶׁעָמְדָה

וְהִיא שֶׁעָמְדָה is generally understood to refer to the *promise* of God in the form of the covenant, about which we have just spoken. Others say it refers to the Torah. A more homiletical interpretation sees וְהִיא שֶׁעָמְדָה standing for the wine cup, which we raise, and specifically for the law against drinking gentile wine. This prohibition, limiting social intercourse with the non-Jews, has helped prevent intermarriage and assimilation throughout our history. It has thus preserved us as a people.

Raise the cup of wine, cover the matzah, and say:

This promise made to our forefathers holds true also for us. For more than once have they risen against us to destroy us; in every generation they rise against us and seek our destruction. But the Holy One, blessed be He, saves us from their hands.

וְהִיא שֶׁעָמְדָה לַאֲבוֹתֵינוּ וְלָנוּ. שֶׁלֹּא אֶחָד בִּלְבָד, עָמַד עָלֵינוּ לְכַלּוֹתֵנוּ. אֶלָּא שֶׁבְּכָל דּוֹר וָדוֹר, עוֹמְדִים עָלֵינוּ לְכַלּוֹתֵנוּ. וְהַקָּדוֹשׁ בָּרוּךְ הוּא מַצִּילֵנוּ מִיָּדָם:

Put down the cup, uncover the matzah, and continue:

The Mishnah teaches that a particular biblical passage in Deuteronomy (26:5–8) be expounded during the Seder as part of *maggid*. Torah study in its most pristine form involves the study of a biblical text with its midrashic explication. In other words, we are bidden to study the Written Law with the interpretation of the Oral Law. This union between תּוֹרָה שֶׁבִּכְתָב and תּוֹרָה שֶׁבְּעַל פֶּה is fundamental to Jewish life and practice. On this night of Torah study we indeed take a biblical text and explicate it with the help of the Midrash, the embodiment of the Oral Torah. This method of study actually began with the Four Questions, which, as we have mentioned, are also based on Torah passages.

The opening words צֵא וּלְמַד, "go out and learn," are striking. One generally studies at home or in school. But Jewish study must also express itself "outside." It is not sufficient that only the study house or the home be permeated with Jewish feeling and expression. The Torah must affect the student so that when he leaves his study, he remains the most legitimate expression of Torah. "Go out and learn"—make sure that your learning accompanies you wherever you go. The psalmist sings, "Go children, listen to me as I teach you how to fear God" (Ps. 34:12). One might expect David to have said "*Come* children" rather than "*Go* children." The fear of God must accompany us everywhere—especially when we go out. This is quite the opposite of what the *maskilim* of the nineteenth century taught when they cried, "Be a Jew in your home and a human being in the street." The proper Jewish view is that we be Jews and human beings both at home *and* in the street.

אֲרַמִּי אֹבֵד אָבִי

The passage beginning with צֵא וּלְמַד מַה בִּקֵּשׁ לָבָן הָאֲרַמִּי is a rabbinic explication of a *parashah* in *Ki Tavo* (Deut. 26:5–8). The obvious question that begs asking is why the Haggadah chose a biblical section in Deuteronomy dealing with *bikkurim* (first fruits) to use as the basis for studying the Exodus. Why not go to the Book of Exodus, which relates directly how we left Egypt?

The solution is that the story in Exodus is told in the third person while the Deuteronomic recital is in the first person. The speaker in Deuteronomy is a native of the Land of Israel, a farmer bringing the first fruits of his field to the priest at the Sanctuary. Though the Exodus from Egypt may already be far in the past, and though his verbal recitation is a formal one, this man fully identifies with his people and its history. Like him each pilgrim throughout the centuries appropriates the wandering Aramean as his father and acknowledges the slaves of Egypt as his people who were redeemed. This identification with the past is placed in the sharpest focus by the individual's speaking in the plural, traditionally the way in which the speaker addressing God asserts that he is part of the Jewish community. Expressing himself this way, the Jew becomes a corporate personality; all of Jewish history lives in and through him. None of these notions are present in a third-person, narrative-type recitation of the event. That explains why the compilers of the Haggadah chose biblical verses that speak in the first person about what happened to the Jewish people. In this way the Seder effects the total identification of the celebrant with his past and his people.

There is a famous story about Rabbi Israel Salanter, who founded the Musar movement in the nineteenth century. During one of Lithuania's freezing winters, his yeshivah had no money to buy fuel and the students had to study in the numbing cold. Early one morning, dressed in a warm fur coat, Rabbi Yisroel went to the home of a wealthy, but not very philanthropic, householder. Still in his dressing gown, the man invited the rabbi in, but the sage remained in the doorway and, seemingly unaware that the householder was shivering from the cold, began a lengthy talmudic discourse. The host's teeth were chattering and before long his lips had turned blue. Thinking he was about to faint, the man finally interrupted the rabbi and persuaded him to come in. As they warmed themselves before the stove, Rabbi Yisroel continued, "I am sure that you are wondering about my strange conduct. The students are freezing; we need money for fuel. If I had asked you to help while you were warm and comfortable, you would not have even begun to understand what it means to study in an unheated room in sub-zero weather. Now that you feel what they feel, I am sure that you will help me." And indeed, the wealthy man provided the fuel for the *beit midrash* as long as he lived.

Similarly, if we are to understand the message of Passover night, we must identify personally and directly with the Jews who left

Egypt, testifying that the great events of Jewish history happened to each of us, that they course through our blood, and that we are one with our ancestors. Only through this total identification with the Jewish people can we ensure the historical continuity of Judaism and Jewry.

There is a second reason why this particular portion is explicated on the Seder night. These are the words of a Jew bringing his offering of thanksgiving to God. His is an expression of *hakorat hatov*—an acknowledgment of God's goodness. On hearing this recitation, we too are aroused by feelings of *hakorat hatov* for redeeming our fathers, as He redeems us in every generation and will ultimately redeem the world. By reciting this passage we also learn that redemption imposes obligation—that the best must be offered to God. On the Seder night we not only remember and re-experience, but we also commit ourselves in gratitude and faith to be true to our Redeemer and His Law.

Finally this passage from Deuteronomy contains a reference to the destination of the Jews after their exodus from Egypt. We were delivered from slavery to serve the Almighty in our own homeland at the Holy Temple.

The Role of Laban

The Haggadah's interpretation of אֲרַמִּי אֹבֵד אָבִי diverges from the plain meaning of the verse. According to the latter, the reference is to Jacob (or perhaps Abraham), who was a wandering Aramean, since his family stemmed from Aram and throughout his lifetime he was constantly on the move. He escaped from Esau and later from Laban. He fled from Shechem after his sons avenged their sister's honor. In his later years he left Canaan for Egypt. He is the prototype of the wandering Jew.

The Midrash—and the Haggadah—read the verse differently. "An Aramean tried to destroy my father." אֹבֵד is understood as a transitive verb ("to destroy") rather than as a participle ("wandering"). The Aramean is Laban, who lived in Aram and is clearly associated with this land by the Torah. Apparently, the Midrash was reluctant to have our forefather called an "Aramean." The epithet was more appropriate to Jacob's uncle, Laban.

Why does the Haggadah mention Laban? What has he to do with the Exodus? Apparently the Haggadah teaches us through Laban's example that Jews ought to fear the enemy within as much or even more than the enemy without. While non-Jewish persecutors, such as Pharaoh, have taken their toll of Jewish lives throughout history, even more Jews have been lost through the blandishments of the Labans of the world. Those presumably close to us—our "family"—have caused more danger to the Jewish community through the scourge of assimilation. Their kiss has been the kiss of death. As the Haggadah explains, Laban, the enemy who appears as a friend, intended to destroy all, men and women. He was thus more dangerous than Pharaoh—the avowed and identifiable foe—who directed his attempts only at the males. Even Jacob did not escape unharmed from Laban, for the latter's feigned solicitude toward the former left a mark, as we shall soon see.

When Jacob first left his father's home, he dreamt a dream of a ladder uniting heaven and earth, with angels ascending and descending and God standing at its head confirming Jacob's faith. This was the dream of a man with great spiritual wealth. But after twenty years of living close to Laban, Jacob now dreams of spotted and speckled and striped calves—of material success and prosperity. He dreams of the stock market, as it were. And so the angel of the Lord appears to Jacob in a dream to tell him, "I see all that Laban has done to you" (Gen. 31:12). By living closely with one who is not God-fearing, Jacob has become somewhat assimilated. And so the angel warns him to return to his roots—to the land of his fathers. Despite Laban's pleas that "your children are my children," Jacob realizes the danger and leaves him before it is too late.

While Jacob essentially avoided assimilation, the Israelites in Egypt two generations later were not so fortunate. Initially the Jewish experience in Egypt contained a measure of sweetness. Just like Laban the Aramean, the Egyptians accepted us, enabled us to flourish and to become successful. The extent of Jewish assimilation into Egyptian society is hinted at in the very beginning of the Book of Exodus (1:7). וּבְנֵי יִשְׂרָאֵל פָּרוּ וַיִּשְׁרְצוּ וַיִּרְבּוּ וַיַּעַצְמוּ בִּמְאֹד מְאֹד—"And the Israelites were fertile and prolific; they multiplied and increased very greatly." The word וַיִּשְׁרְצוּ, which is roughly translated as "were prolific," literally means "swarmed"—like insects and rodents. They swarmed all over Egypt like creeping things—an apparent expression of disgust. The midrash relates that Jews were found everywhere: in the theater, at the circus, in the dance halls—wherever they should not have been. Allured by the openness of the culture, they forgot their origins. To put it another way, they were being kissed to death.

Ironically, what saved them was the ascent of a new monarch who openly declared his hatred for the Israelites. By persecuting them, he reminded them of their particular ancestry, which they could not abandon or forsake. When the Jews forget their faith, God reminds them by sending the gentiles.

To summarize, the persecution of the Jews resulted from their courtship with assimilation. By succumbing to the initial "sweetness" of their neighbors, the Jews brought upon themselves the Egyptian oppression.

This unexpected turn of events is commemorated through the mitzvah of *maror*. The preferred vegetable that one takes for this ritual is Romaine lettuce—a product whose leaves are sweet but whose root is bitter. The initial amiability of the Egyptians brought on the later near-destruction of the Jewish people.

Come and learn what Laban the Syrian tried to do to our father Jacob. While Pharaoh decreed only against the males. Laban desired to uproot all. For so it is written: "A Syrian sought to destroy my father; and he went down to Egypt and dwelled there, a handful, few in number. There he became a nation, great, mighty and numerous."

צֵא וּלְמַד, מַה בִּקֵּשׁ לָבָן הָאֲרַמִּי לַעֲשׂוֹת לְיַעֲקֹב אָבִינוּ. שֶׁפַּרְעֹה לֹא גָזַר אֶלָּא עַל־הַזְּכָרִים, וְלָבָן בִּקֵּשׁ לַעֲקֹר אֶת־הַכֹּל. שֶׁנֶּאֱמַר: אֲרַמִּי אֹבֵד אָבִי, וַיֵּרֶד מִצְרַיְמָה, וַיָּגָר שָׁם בִּמְתֵי מְעָט. וַיְהִי שָׁם לְגוֹי גָּדוֹל, עָצוּם וָרָב:

וַיֵּרֶד מִצְרַיְמָה . . . לָגוּר שָׁם

Jacob came to Egypt merely to stay for a short time, but such is the danger of exile that after a while his offspring began to see Egypt as their homeland. It takes only one generation. The Israelites came as members of a single family and grew in numbers as the stars in heaven. Anxious to be respected by the Egyptians, they yielded up every vestige of their Jewishness. They remained distinct physically and economically, but not spiritually.

"He went down to Egypt"— Why did he go down to Egypt? He was compelled by God's decree. "He dwelled there"— this means that Jacob our father did not go down to Egypt to settle there but only to stay for a short while; for so it is said: "And they said to Pharaoh, we have come to dwell in the land because there is no pasture for the flocks of your servants, since the famine is very bad in the land of Canaan; and now let your servants dwell in the land of Goshen."

וַיֵּרֶד מִצְרַיְמָה. אָנוּס עַל־פִּי הַדִּבּוּר. וַיָּגָר שָׁם. מְלַמֵּד שֶׁלֹּא יָרַד יַעֲקֹב אָבִינוּ לְהִשְׁתַּקֵּעַ בְּמִצְרַיִם. אֶלָּא לָגוּר שָׁם. שֶׁנֶּאֱמַר: וַיֹּאמְרוּ אֶל־פַּרְעֹה, לָגוּר בָּאָרֶץ בָּאנוּ, כִּי־אֵין מִרְעֶה לַצֹּאן אֲשֶׁר לַעֲבָדֶיךָ, כִּי־כָבֵד הָרָעָב בְּאֶרֶץ כְּנָעַן. וְעַתָּה, יֵשְׁבוּ־נָא עֲבָדֶיךָ בְּאֶרֶץ גֹּשֶׁן:

"Few in number"—as it is said: "Your forefathers went down into Egypt with seventy persons. Now the Eternal your God has made you as numerous as the stars in heaven."

בִּמְתֵי מְעָט. כְּמָה שֶׁנֶּאֱמַר: בְּשִׁבְעִים נֶפֶשׁ, יָרְדוּ אֲבֹתֶיךָ מִצְרַיְמָה. וְעַתָּה, שָׂמְךָ יְיָ אֱלֹהֶיךָ, כְּכוֹכְבֵי הַשָּׁמַיִם לָרֹב:

וַיְהִי שָׁם לְגוֹי

Israel lived well, increased abundantly, and multiplied. The land was filled with Jews; they occupied the highest professional positions and were found in the highest economic echelons. In Ezekiel's poetic imagery: "I made you thrive like the plants of the field, and you grew big and tall, and attained great charm and perfect form, and your hair grew long" (Ez. 16:7). This is also an apt description of the comfortable life the Jews lived in Spain during the Golden Age and in Germany before the Third Reich. It is the way we Jews are living in the United States. Professionally and economically—and even politically—we have practically reached the pinnacle. As a minority, we have achieved success and prestige far beyond the strength of our numbers. But Jewish history teaches us that the Jew in exile should expect to be toppled from his high position and even to be plunged to the lowest of depths. The end of the verse we have just quoted alludes to the final fall. וְאַתְּ עֵרֹם וְעֶרְיָה can mean that despite their success, the Jews were "naked and bare." From rags to riches could easily become from riches to rags. The Egyptian experience remains as a constant reminder of the precariousness of the condition of the Jewish people in exile.

Our insecurity is the reason that festivals are celebrated for two days in the Diaspora. The Talmud (*Bezah* 4b) explains that in Temple times the date of the new moon (Rosh Ḥodesh) depended on the testimony of witnesses who observed the sliver of the new moon in the skies and then appeared before the Sanhedrin to describe what they had seen. Once their testimony was verified, the judges of the court would declare that day to be Rosh Ḥodesh. Since the Torah ordains that the festivals must be observed on certain specified days of the month, the declaration establishing that a new month had begun also determined the day or days on which the festivals of that month would occur. The Diaspora Jews, however, could not be readily informed of the judges' determination, so they did not know precisely on what day the festivals would fall. Therefore, the Talmud maintains, two days would be celebrated. The problem then rises of explaining the continuation of this *galut* phenomenon even after the adoption of a fixed calendar, which took place already in talmudic times. To this question the Talmud curtly responds: "Maintain the observances of your forebears, for there might come a time when the government will decree [against the Jews] and error [in the calendrical system] will ensue."

As long as the Jew lives in the Diaspora, even his calendar can be taken from him. The situation of the Jew in exile is so precarious that there are places where he may not know when to celebrate the festivals, and it was with this in mind that the rabbis decreed the second festival day regardless of the calendar's adoption. Our persecuted brothers and sisters in the Soviet Union are in exactly this kind of predicament. Anyone who has visited that country knows how fervently they besiege Jewish tourists with requests for a *luaḥ*, a simple little Jewish calendar that will enable them to observe the holy days of the Jewish year.

"And there he became a nation"—from this we learn that Israel became a distinct nation in Egypt.

וַיְהִי שָׁם לְגוֹי. מְלַמֵּד שֶׁהָיוּ יִשְׂרָאֵל מְצֻיָּנִים שָׁם:

"Great and mighty"—as it is said: "And the children of Israel were fruitful and increased and multiplied and became very strong and numerous, so that the land was full of them."

גָּדוֹל עָצוּם. כְּמָה שֶׁנֶּאֱמַר: וּבְנֵי יִשְׂרָאֵל, פָּרוּ וַיִּשְׁרְצוּ, וַיִּרְבּוּ וַיַּעַצְמוּ, בִּמְאֹד מְאֹד. וַתִּמָּלֵא הָאָרֶץ אֹתָם:

"And numerous"—as it is said: "I have increased you as the growth of the field, and you have become numerous and grown big and reached to excellence in beauty. You are fully grown, yet you remained naked and bare."

וָרָב. כְּמָה שֶׁנֶּאֱמַר: רְבָבָה כְּצֶמַח הַשָּׂדֶה נְתַתִּיךְ, וַתִּרְבִּי, וַתִּגְדְּלִי, וַתָּבֹאִי בַּעֲדִי עֲדָיִים. שָׁדַיִם נָכֹנוּ, וּשְׂעָרֵךְ צִמֵּחַ, וְאַתְּ עֵרֹם וְעֶרְיָה:

וַיָּרֵעוּ אוֹתָנוּ הַמִּצְרִים ·

We find three different interpretations of this phrase. First, "the Egyptians treated us wickedly." This is the widely assumed meaning and is based on the assumption that וַיָּרֵעוּ means "they did evil to."

A second interpretation—assuming וַיָּרֵעוּ to be a causative (*hiphil*)—reads it as "the Egyptians ascribed evil things to us." They made us out to be wicked. Every anti-Semite tries to demonstrate that there is a legitimate basis for his hatred of the Jews, thereby hiding his own intolerance and prejudice. He first denigrates us and vilifies us to justify his oppression. He tries to show that the Jews are clannish and untrustworthy—interested only in themselves and their coreligionists. The Egyptians followed this script; they were the first anti-Semites.

The third interpretation considers וַיָּרֵעוּ as derived from the word

רֵעַ, "friend." Thus וַיָּרֵעוּ means "they befriended us." It was a ploy to enable their anti-Semitic designs to be successful. Pharaoh understood that he had to begin slowly. The Israelites were much too numerous for him. So he said, "Let us deal shrewdly with them lest they increase and, in the event of a war, join our enemies in fighting against us and gaining ascendancy over the country" (Ex. 1:10). He espouses the familiar canard of the disloyalty of the Jew, who has no national roots and no national loyalties, a charge that Haman used so effectively a thousand years later. Pharaoh's argument that the Jews are a treacherous people—who are and remain foreigners—was the same argument that was used by the Nazis despite the immense contributions Jews had made to German culture. The Jews, as a result of the Nazi charges, were degraded and expelled from all trades and professions. They were considered Jewish bacilli infecting the German body—social and cultural degenerates who had to be cleared out or subdued by all possible means. Pharaoh too thought along these lines.

To continue with the third interpretation of וַיָּרֵעוּ, the Jews would not willingly become slaves, and Pharaoh could not adopt a policy of force because the Jews were too numerous and had "spread throughout the land." There had to be a way to obviate the possibility of a Jewish uprising, to make the Jews cooperate with their own enslavement. Pharaoh's cunning advisors had the remedy: they would lure the Jews into slavery by appealing to their patriotism. According to the Midrash, Pharaoh declared something akin to a National Works Project. He himself initiated it by making a few bricks, and the Jews, always willing to out-Egyptian the Egyptians, began to work day and night, week in and week out, month in and month out, to further the Egyptian "national effort." The Egyptians began slowly. They declared that they would work with their Jewish friends. Gradually the Egyptians changed their methods. But once the Jews started working for them, they could no longer stop, for their loyalty would be questioned. Slowly but surely what began as a volunteer effort turned into forced labor replete with overlords and taskmasters. A kind of *Judenrat* was put into place. When the Jews continued to increase, Pharaoh's oppression became more severe. A "Final Solution" was adopted: to kill the Jewish males as they were born. Only the hand of God saved us from our erstwhile "friends."

"And the Egyptians did evil unto us and they made us suffer. They set upon us hard work." "And the Egyptians did evil unto us"—as it is said in the Bible: "Come, let us deal craftily with them, lest they increase yet more, and it may be that when war occurs they will be added to our enemies and fight against us and go out of the land."

וַיָּרֵעוּ אֹתָנוּ הַמִּצְרִים וַיְעַנּוּנוּ. וַיִּתְּנוּ עָלֵינוּ עֲבֹדָה קָשָׁה: וַיָּרֵעוּ אֹתָנוּ הַמִּצְרִים, כְּמָה שֶׁנֶּאֱמַר: הָבָה נִתְחַכְּמָה לוֹ. פֶּן־יִרְבֶּה וְהָיָה כִּי־תִקְרֶאנָה מִלְחָמָה, וְנוֹסַף גַּם־ הוּא עַל־שֹׂנְאֵינוּ, וְנִלְחַם־בָּנוּ וְעָלָה מִן־הָאָרֶץ:

"And they made us suffer"—as the Bible relates: "So the Egyptians set taskmasters over them in order to oppress them with their burdens; and they built Pithom and Raamses as store-cities for Pharaoh." "And they set upon us hard work"—as the Bible states:

וַיְעַנּוּנוּ. כְּמָה שֶׁנֶּאֱמַר: וַיָּשִׂימוּ עָלָיו שָׂרֵי מִסִּים לְמַעַן עַנֹּתוֹ בְּסִבְלֹתָם: וַיִּבֶן עָרֵי מִסְכְּנוֹת לְפַרְעֹה, אֶת־פִּתֹם וְאֶת־רַעַמְסֵס: וַיִּתְּנוּ עָלֵינוּ עֲבֹדָה קָשָׁה. כְּמָה שֶׁנֶּאֱמַר: וַיַּעֲבִדוּ מִצְרַיִם אֶת־בְּנֵי יִשְׂרָאֵל בְּפָרֶךְ:

"And Egypt made the children of Israel labor rigorously."

וַנִּצְעַק אֶל ה׳

In Exodus 2:23 the Torah tells us that the Jews began to cry out only after the old Pharaoh died and a new king arose, although the slavery and oppression had started earlier. Why did the groaning not start earlier?

According to one tradition, the "new king who knew not Joseph" was as harsh as the first one. But at least while the old Pharaoh was alive—the one who knew Joseph—there was hope that he might change his decree against the Jews, for as he made the policy so could he change it. But once he died and a new Pharaoh took over, they knew that the evil decree had become part and parcel of Egyptian law and life. According to a second interpretation, the second Pharaoh was a little more lenient than the first, so that groaning was at least permitted. Sometimes the oppression is so great that it is impossible even to cry out. Before the new Pharaoh discovered all of his royal powers there was an instant of respite in which the Jews could groan.

The Israelites, however, did not necessarily cry out to God. "They cried, and their cry ascended to God" (Ex. 2:23). It was like the cry of an animal in pain; it was not directed to anyone in particular.° So too the Jews in Egypt, not yet God-conscious, lifted their voices and bemoaned their fate. God heard them and hearkened to them.

"So we cried unto the Eternal, the God of our fathers, and the Eternal heard our voice, and He saw our affliction, and our burden, and our oppression."

וַנִּצְעַק אֶל־יְיָ אֱלֹהֵי אֲבֹתֵינוּ, וַיִּשְׁמַע יְיָ אֶת־קֹלֵנוּ, וַיַּרְא אֶת־עָנְיֵנוּ, וְאֶת־עֲמָלֵנוּ, וְאֶת־לַחֲצֵנוּ:

"So we cried unto the Eternal, the God of our fathers"—as the Bible recounts: "And it came to pass in the course of those many days that the King of Egypt died, and the children of Israel moaned because of their servitude and cried out, and their outcry came up unto God."

וַנִּצְעַק אֶל־יְיָ אֱלֹהֵי אֲבוֹתֵינוּ. כְּמָה שֶׁנֶּאֱמַר: וַיְהִי בַיָּמִים הָרַבִּים הָהֵם, וַיָּמָת מֶלֶךְ מִצְרַיִם, וַיֵּאָנְחוּ בְנֵי־יִשְׂרָאֵל מִן־הָעֲבֹדָה וַיִּזְעָקוּ. וַתַּעַל שַׁוְעָתָם אֶל־הָאֱלֹהִים מִן־הָעֲבֹדָה:

וַיִּשְׁמַע ה׳ אֶת קוֹלֵנוּ

When God heard our cry, He knew that Israel had to be redeemed if it were to remain alive at all. God was really waiting for this cry. We *must* cry out to our Father in heaven—in the form of prayer—for when we do the Almighty will hear. Reb Moshe Leib Sassover (1745–1807) came home from the synagogue one Passover

° In Deut. 26:7 it is written that the cries were directed to God, but perhaps those were the cries that came later—after Moses appeared on the scene and made the Jews aware of God's promise to deliver them.

night and told his wife and his students that he would not begin the Seder until his small child had awakened. Midnight passed. The child did not awaken and it was too late to begin the Seder. Reb Moshe Leib Sassover turned to the Almighty God: "Master of the Universe, I waited for my child to wake up by himself, but he kept on sleeping. Don't wait for the Jews to wake up by themselves; their oppression is too great to expect this of them. You must wake them so that the Seder of redemption can begin."

"And the Eternal heard our voice"—as the Bible tells: "And God heard their groaning, and God remembered His covenant with Abraham, with Isaac and with Jacob."

וַיִּשְׁמַע יְיָ אֶת־קוֹלֵנוּ. כְּמָה שֶׁנֶּאֱמַר: וַיִּשְׁמַע אֱלֹהִים אֶת־נַאֲקָתָם. וַיִּזְכֹּר אֱלֹהִים אֶת־בְּרִיתוֹ, אֶת־אַבְרָהָם, אֶת־יִצְחָק וְאֶת־יַעֲקֹב:

וַיַּרְא אֶת עָנְיֵנוּ

Va-yar et anyenu refers to *derekh eretz*, the separation of husband and wife and the suspension of marital relations. The proof-text is striking: "God looked upon the Children of Israel and God knew." The text does not indicate what God saw. How does the Midrash then deduce that the Jews suffered sexual oppression?

There are two kinds of oppression: active oppression, where the persecutor's evil deeds are nakedly visible and the suffering is physical; and silent oppression, where the suffering is mental and psychological. The Jews in Egypt were victims of both types. The active, physical persecution they endured is explicitly mentioned in the Torah. Not so the mental anguish. Here the Midrash refers to it by focusing upon the intrusion of the oppressor into the bedroom of the Jewish slave.

Sexuality is a basic human drive. It binds together husband and wife and is the most positive affirmation of the future—through the creation of progeny. But when a person is enslaved, when his time is not his own, when he has worked at backbreaking labor for impossibly long hours—comes evening he falls on his bed exhausted. He has not the physical strength or the mental concentration to engage in sexual relations, and he lacks the normal desire to produce offspring. וַיַּרְא אֱלֹקִים ("And God saw") apparently refers to a kind of suffering that only God can see and know. Thus it is followed by וַיֵּדַע אֱלֹקִים ("and God knew"). The Midrash then deduces that the reference is not to active oppression, which is visible to all, but to the silent mental and emotional anguish that is associated with sexual deprivation.

The Role of the Women

When the Sanctuary was being built in the desert, the women brought their mirrors to be melted down to be made into lavers for the priests and Levites, and these were gladly accepted. One might wonder whether it was not sacrilegious to make use of mirrors, the symbol of vanity, in the Temple of the Lord. The Midrash relates that when the Jews in Egypt came home at night exhausted, wanting nothing else but a few hours of fitful sleep, with nothing to look forward to but another day of backbreaking labor, their wives would look into their mirrors to make themselves attractive so that sexual relationships would continue. Despite the miserable conditions, the women urged their husbands to have children and not to lose faith in the future. Therefore, these mirrors were holy and deserved their place in the Sanctuary of God. בִּזְכוּת נָשִׁים צִדְקָנִיּוֹת—by the merit of these righteous women, says the Talmud, was Israel redeemed from Egypt (*Sotah* 11b).

This point is illustrated by another tradition, which relates that Amram, the father of Moses, was at one time head of the Sanhedrin. When Pharaoh decreed that the male offspring be killed, Amram said that it was futile for the Israelites to beget children. Forthwith he ceased to have intercourse with his wife, Jochebed. Thereupon all the Israelites arose and separated themselves from their wives. But his daughter Miriam protested his decision. "Your decree is more severe than that of Pharaoh, for the king decreed only concerning male children, but your decree affects both males and females alike. Besides, Pharaoh being wicked, there is some doubt whether his proclamation will be fulfilled, but you are righteous and your decree will be fulfilled." So Amram took his wife back, as did the others (*Exodus Rabbah* 1:13). The righteous and sensitive advice of Miriam was indirectly responsible for the birth of Moses and the later redemption of the Jewish people.

The importance of bearing children cannot be underestimated. In a sense the perseverance of the Jews in Egypt and their efforts to multiply and propagate, despite all the oppression and travail they endured, brought on the Exodus. It was the greatest indication of their faith in the future—and in a better world. This can best be illustrated by a fascinating incident recorded in the Bible.

The Book of Genesis (19:30–38) tells the dreadful story of Abraham's nephew, Lot, who together with his two daughters was saved from the destruction of Sodom and Gomorrah. The daughters, thinking that the world had come to an end and concerned about the continuance of the human race, got their father drunk so as to have sexual relations with him. One of the children born of these incestuous unions was named Moab (מוֹאָב) from מֵאָב, "from father." In one of the ironies of biblical history, a descendant of Moab—Ruth—converted to Judaism, was married to Boaz, and became the great-grandmother of King David, ancestor of the Messiah. Is it not strange that the hope of all Israel should have such an ignominious heritage—that he should be the product of a forbidden union?

We can perceive the importance of this genealogical relationship if we remember that the destruction of Sodom and Gomorrah was akin to the Holocaust in our own time. According to the Midrash, Lot and his daughters truly believed that they were the only people left on earth. But if one Holocaust had occurred, another was equally likely. Lot's daughters had every reason to believe that if they were to bear children, these children would be destroyed, just as their contemporaries had been. Nevertheless, the two women expressed their belief in the future of humanity in the only way they knew. They gave birth. They sought to ensure the survival of mankind by bringing forth another generation. While they were actually in error about humanity's destruction, their intention was to preserve mankind in the hope that there would be a better future. Only if one believes in humanity can one believe in the Messiah, for our vision of the messianic era is one of perfected mankind. Hence, by their deed the daughters of Lot attained the merit that through them would be born Ruth, the progenitrix of the Messiah of Israel, who would bring redemption to the entire world, thus fulfilling the aim and purpose of all history.

The Jews in Egypt, as well, because they believed in the future, merited redemption. In recent history, the Jews merited the land of Israel because even in the concentration camps they continued to proclaim their belief in the Jewish future, and after their liberation they continued to have children. Can we today, living in relative comfort in America or in Israel, have less faith than our fathers? Can we afford to cut our birthrate in half as some misguided souls have advised, and thereby jeopardize our demographic survival? Can we view with equanimity the abortion rate in Israel, a country that is constantly begging for *olim* and that desperately needs young people? We as a nation have always prided ourselves on upholding the sanctity of life as well as the affirmation of life through the mitzvah of begetting children. Only such an expression of faith in the Jewish future can ensure the survival of the Jewish present.

"And He saw our affliction"— this phrase suggests the enforced separation of husband and wife under Pharaoh's persecution, as it is written: "And God saw the children of Israel and God understood their plight."

וַיַּרְא אֶת־עָנְיֵנוּ. זוֹ פְּרִישׁוּת דֶּרֶךְ אֶרֶץ. כְּמָה שֶׁנֶּאֱמַר: וַיַּרְא אֱלֹהִים אֶת־בְּנֵי יִשְׂרָאֵל. וַיֵּדַע אֱלֹהִים:

"And our burden"—this recalls the drowning of the male children, as it is said: "Every son that is born you shall cast into the Nile, but every daughter you may keep alive."

וְאֶת־עֲמָלֵנוּ. אֵלּוּ הַבָּנִים. כְּמָה שֶׁנֶּאֱמַר: כָּל־הַבֵּן הַיִּלּוֹד הַיְאֹרָה תַּשְׁלִיכֻהוּ, וְכָל־הַבַּת תְּחַיּוּן:

"And our oppression"—this refers to crushing our lives, as the Bible says: "And I have seen the oppression with which the Egyptians are oppressing them."

וְאֶת־לַחֲצֵנוּ. זוֹ הַדְּחַק. כְּמָה שֶׁנֶּאֱמַר: וְגַם־רָאִיתִי אֶת־הַלַּחַץ, אֲשֶׁר מִצְרַיִם לֹחֲצִים אֹתָם:

"And the Eternal brought us forth from Egypt, with a strong hand, and with an outstretched arm, and with great fear, and with signs and wonders."

וַיּוֹצִאֵנוּ יְיָ מִמִּצְרַיִם, בְּיָד חֲזָקָה, וּבִזְרֹעַ נְטוּיָה, וּבְמֹרָא גָּדֹל. וּבְאֹתוֹת וּבְמֹפְתִים:

וַיּוֹצִאֵנוּ ה׳ מִמִּצְרַיִם — אֲנִי וְלֹא מַלְאָךְ . . . אֲנִי וְלֹא שָׂרָף . . . אֲנִי וְלֹא שָׁלִיחַ

Why does the text so repeatedly emphasize that God alone was responsible for the Exodus? First and most obviously, this is a statement directed against Christianity. We believe in pure monotheism; God did not and does not have to operate through any other being. There is a direct interaction between God and man. This is the meaning of Jacob's dream of the ladder that connects heaven and earth. There is no need for demigods, for we have a personal relationship with our Father in Heaven and the ability and opportunity to comunicate with Him directly.

Second, the emphasis on God's role in bringing the Jews out of Egypt is to deny any central role to Moses. Indeed his name does not appear in the Haggadah unless it is part of a quotation or a prayer. The authors of the Haggadah wanted to make absolutely certain that later generations, not having a leader like Moses, would not feel unworthy of redemption. God alone is the hero of the Exodus, and just as God is eternal, so is His promise of redemption. No human being can take full credit for our redemption. To the Almighty alone can we ascribe this historical deed, as it is written: "I am the Lord thy God who took you out of the land of Egypt." As He redeemed our fathers from Egyptian bondage, so will He redeem us and our children—if we are worthy.

It is interesting to note that the burial place of Moses was never revealed in the Bible and remains undisclosed to this day. Perhaps the Torah is thereby teaching us that succeeding generations dare not make a shrine of our prophet's tomb. While on the subject, there is also another lesson to be derived from the curious fact that Moses' burial site is unknown. In truth our leader never died. His Torah and his vision of a redeeming God live on as long as Jews continue to study his words. This is what the Rabbis mean when they say that a great sage never dies. He lives on through his learning and scholarship. Moses, our teacher par excellence, is very much alive, and, therefore, no one can find his burial place.

"And the Eternal brought us forth from Egypt"—not by a ministering angel, not by a fiery angel, not by a messen-

וַיּוֹצִיאֵנוּ יְיָ מִמִּצְרַיִם. לֹא עַל־יְדֵי מַלְאָךְ. וְלֹא עַל־יְדֵי שָׂרָף. וְלֹא עַל־יְדֵי שָׁלִיחַ. אֶלָּא הַקָּדוֹשׁ בָּרוּךְ

ger, but by Himself, in His glory, did the Holy One, blessed be He, as the Bible records: "And I will pass through the land of Egypt on that night, and I will smite all the first-born in the land of Egypt from man to beast, and against all the gods of Egypt I will execute judgments. It is I, the Eternal."

הוּא בִּכְבוֹדוֹ וּבְעַצְמוֹ. שֶׁנֶּאֱמַר: וְעָבַרְתִּי בְאֶרֶץ־מִצְרַיִם בַּלַּיְלָה הַזֶּה. וְהִכֵּיתִי כָל־בְּכוֹר בְּאֶרֶץ מִצְרַיִם מֵאָדָם וְעַד־בְּהֵמָה. וּבְכָל־אֱלֹהֵי מִצְרַיִם, אֶעֱשֶׂה שְׁפָטִים, אֲנִי יְיָ:

"And I will pass through the land of Egypt"—I and not a ministering angel; "and I will smite the first-born in the land of Egypt"—I and not a fiery angel; "and against all the gods of Egypt I will execute judgments"—I and not a messenger; "I, the Eternal"—I and no other.

וְעָבַרְתִּי בְאֶרֶץ־מִצְרַיִם בַּלַּיְלָה הַזֶּה, אֲנִי וְלֹא מַלְאָךְ. וְהִכֵּיתִי כָל־בְּכוֹר בְּאֶרֶץ־מִצְרַיִם, אֲנִי וְלֹא שָׂרָף. וּבְכָל־אֱלֹהֵי מִצְרַיִם אֶעֱשֶׂה שְׁפָטִים, אֲנִי וְלֹא הַשָּׁלִיחַ. אֲנִי יְיָ, אֲנִי הוּא וְלֹא אַחֵר:

"With a strong hand"—this refers to the cattle plague, as it is said in the Bible: "Behold, the hand of the Eternal will be against the cattle that is in the field, against the horses, the donkeys, the camels, the oxen and the sheep, a very grievous plague."

בְּיָד חֲזָקָה. זוֹ הַדֶּבֶר. כְּמָה שֶׁנֶּאֱמַר: הִנֵּה יַד־יְיָ הוֹיָה, בְּמִקְנְךָ אֲשֶׁר בַּשָּׂדֶה, בַּסּוּסִים בַּחֲמֹרִים בַּגְּמַלִּים, בַּבָּקָר וּבַצֹּאן. דֶּבֶר כָּבֵד מְאֹד:

"And with an outstretched arm"—this refers to the sword, as the Bible states: "His sword drawn in His hand, outstretched against Jerusalem."

וּבִזְרֹעַ נְטוּיָה זוֹ הַחֶרֶב. כְּמָה שֶׁנֶּאֱמַר: וְחַרְבּוֹ שְׁלוּפָה בְּיָדוֹ, נְטוּיָה עַל־יְרוּשָׁלָיִם:

"And with great fear"—this refers to the Revelation of God to Israel, as it is said: "Has any

וּבְמֹרָא גָּדוֹל. זוֹ גִּלּוּי שְׁכִינָה. כְּמָה שֶׁנֶּאֱמַר: אוֹ הֲנִסָּה אֱלֹהִים,

god ever tried to go and remove one nation from the midst of another nation, with trials, with signs and with wonders, and with battle, and with strong hand and outstretched arm, and with great fear, as all that the Eternal your God did for you in Egypt before your eyes?"

לָבוֹא לָקַחַת לוֹ גוֹי מִקֶּרֶב גּוֹי, בְּמַסֹּת בְּאֹתֹת וּבְמוֹפְתִים וּבְמִלְחָמָה, וּבְיָד חֲזָקָה וּבִזְרוֹעַ נְטוּיָה, וּבְמוֹרָאִים גְּדֹלִים. כְּכֹל אֲשֶׁר־עָשָׂה לָכֶם, יְיָ אֱלֹהֵיכֶם, בְּמִצְרַיִם לְעֵינֶיךָ:

וּבְאוֹתוֹת — זֶה הַמַּטֶּה

U-ve'otot—zeh ha-mateh refers to the staff of Moses. What is so special about Moses' shepherd staff that it merits special attention in the Haggadah? The Midrash has many stories about the signs and wonders Moses performed with his staff. At the burning bush, God endowed the staff with wonder-working capabilities to provide Moses with the kind of authority that would impress Pharaoh. The Almighty bade Moses cast his staff to the ground, where it turned into a snake. The Zohar relates that Moses immediately recognized it as the aboriginal snake from the Garden of Eden and recoiled from it, knowing it to be the *Yetzer Hara*—the evil impulse. "Then the Lord said to Moses, 'Put out your hand and grasp it by the tail'—he put out his hand and seized it, and it became a staff in his hand" (Ex. 4:2-4). Thus, helped and encouraged by God, Moses took hold of the evil impulse and made it a means for Divine service. Man has the ability to utilize even the "evil" within him for positive results. By subduing and controlling our impulses, we can turn an active, creative, but unbridled force into a means for good. Our ability to do this is the true secret of personal redemption.

"And with signs"—this refers to the rod of Moses, as it is said: "And thou, Moses, shalt take in thy hand this rod wherewith thou shalt do the signs."

וּבְאוֹתוֹת. זֶה הַמַּטֶּה. כְּמָה שֶׁנֶּאֱמַר: וְאֶת־הַמַּטֶּה הַזֶּה, תִּקַּח בְּיָדֶךָ. אֲשֶׁר תַּעֲשֶׂה־בּוֹ אֶת־הָאֹתֹת:

When at God's command Moses raised his staff and struck the water of the Nile, *all* the waters in Egypt turned into blood (Ex. 7:19 ff.). While this tradition has literal meaning, it also contains a deep symbolic message. The water turning into blood refers to the blood of Jewish commitment: the blood of the paschal sacrifice and the blood of circumcision. The Israelites needed a dual sign of blood to demonstrate their devotion to the Almighty. When the Jews sacrificed the lamb, an animal the Egyptians worshipped, they expressed their dedication to God as the only Lord of the world. When they took a few drops of blood from the organ of propagation of an eight-day-old child, they indicated that they also wanted their children to follow in the faith of the parents and were dedicating themselves to this task. Being a Jew means being willing to put your life on the line for your faith; being a Jew means being linked to the fate of your people—even to the point of giving your blood.

History has shown that Jewish commitment and devotion to God have not come cheap. We have had to pay for them in blood over and over again. The prophet Joel already foresaw this. He speaks of the ultimate redemption in terms of "blood, fire, and pillars of smoke" (Joel 3:3). Fire and pillars of smoke recall Israel's wandering through the desert toward Mount Sinai, led by a pillar of smoke by day and a column of fire by night. Clouds and smoke cause haze. We cannot always see God clearly. That is why commitment and faith—symbolized by blood—are so crucial. As the Rabbis were so well aware, only that for which the Jews were ready to give up their lives was preserved in the long run. "Easy come, easy go," to use a cliché. Jewish faith and belief in God endured because it was worth dying for. As the Exodus depended on our readiness for self-sacrifice, so too the final redemption will require this kind of commitment—symbolized by blood.

"And wonders"—this refers to the plague of blood, as it is written in Scripture: "I will put wonders in heaven and on earth:

וּבְמֹפְתִים. זֶה הַדָּם. כְּמָה שֶׁנֶּאֱמַר: וְנָתַתִּי מוֹפְתִים, בַּשָּׁמַיִם וּבָאָרֶץ.

Spill three drops of wine:

דָּם. וָאֵשׁ. וְתִימְרוֹת עָשָׁן:

1—BLOOD   2—FIRE   3—PILLARS OF SMOKE."

Another interpretation is as follows:

"With a strong hand"—refers to two plagues; "with an outstretched arm"—two; "with great terror"—two; "with signs"—two; and "with wonders" refers to two plagues.

דָּבָר אַחֵר. בְּיָד חֲזָקָה שְׁתַּיִם. וּבִזְרֹעַ נְטוּיָה שְׁתַּיִם. וּבְמֹרָא גָּדֹל שְׁתַּיִם. וּבְאֹתוֹת שְׁתַּיִם. וּבְמֹפְתִים שְׁתַּיִם: אֵלּוּ עֶשֶׂר מַכּוֹת שֶׁהֵבִיא הַקָּדוֹשׁ בָּרוּךְ הוּא עַל־הַמִּצְרִים בְּמִצְרָיִם. וְאֵלּוּ הֵן:

Thus we have the ten plagues that the Holy One, blessed be He, brought upon the Egyptians in Egypt; and they are as follows:

The Plagues

According to Jewish tradition, when each of the plagues is counted, we dip our little finger into the wine and spill a drop of it or pour some wine out of the cup. This symbolizes our sadness at the loss of human life—even that of our enemies.

The Midrash recounts that at the parting of the Red Sea, when the Egyptians were drowning, the angels in heaven recited songs of praise to God. The Almighty reproved them, saying, "The work of My hands is perishing and you sing praises to Me?" We identify with the underdog even if he was our oppressor. Thus, on this night of celebration we remember that our cup of celebration cannot be full to the brim if our redemption was brought about as a result of the destruction of human beings.

We also spill some wine when the three acronyms of R. Judah are read. The Haggadah commentators delight in trying to explain the significance of those acronyms. Most likely they were invented to indicate that the plagues occurred at three different levels, which represent different aspects of Divine mastery over nature and the world. Blood, frogs, and lice affected the ground: the blood, the

Nile River; the frogs, the swamplands surrounding them; and the lice, the solid earth. Wild beasts, pestilence, and boils affected those who lived upon the land. Hail, locusts, and darkness involved the atmosphere. The slaying of the firstborn taught that our God is also the Lord over life and death.

It was important for Pharaoh, who believed that he was a god, to understand that he was creature, not Creator. The lesson was taught to him in stages. R. Judah expresses these stages by grouping the plagues into three words—דְּצַ"ךְ עֲדַ"שׁ בְּאַחַ"ב.

The Sabbath—A Dual Symbol

We Jews are taught often—through the mitzvot—that God alone is the Creator. In particular, this notion is central to the Sabbath.

It is interesting that the Torah offers two reasons for our celebration of the Sabbath. The first is found in Exodus 20:8, where we are commanded to remember the Sabbath to keep it holy because God, who created the heaven and the earth, the sea, and all that is in them in six days, abstained from creativity on the seventh day. The Sabbath is thus a זֵכֶר לְמַעֲשֵׂה בְרֵאשִׁית—a reminder of Creation. It stands as eternal testimony that God is the Creator of the universe.

The second reason is found in Deuteronomy 5:12–15. We are bidden to observe the Sabbath "so that your male and female servants may rest as you do," for we too were slaves in the land of Egypt and the Almighty freed us therefrom. The Sabbath is thus a זֵכֶר לִיצִיאַת מִצְרָיִם. It serves as a celebration of freedom, a day on which we declare that we belong not to a master or to an employer but solely to the Master of the World. It is, therefore, a reminder of the Exodus from Egypt, through which we did in fact achieve our own liberty, as well as an introduction of the concept of freedom to the world at large.

The Sabbath then serves a dual function. It is an affirmation of belief in God as Creator as well as an assertion of man's freedom to serve God.

We can also look upon the Deuteronomic notion of the Sabbath as a corollary to the one in Exodus. Since God is the Creator of all life, we are all His children. As brothers we are bidden to act kindly to each other. No one child of God can enslave another, for we are all equal. No one nation or people can subdue another. We are united by our very creaturehood, which obligates us to serve only God and not each other. Thus we are instructed to observe the Sabbath as a reminder of our freedom. Even our manservant and maidservant may not work on the Sabbath.

Spill a drop of wine for each of the ten plagues:

1.	BLOOD	דָּם.
2.	FROGS	צְפַרְדֵּעַ.
3.	VERMIN	כִּנִּים.
4.	BEASTS	עָרוֹב.
5.	CATTLE DISEASE	דֶּבֶר.
6.	BOILS	שְׁחִין.
7.	HAIL	בָּרָד.
8.	LOCUSTS	אַרְבֶּה.
9.	DARKNESS	חֹשֶׁךְ.
10.	SLAYING OF THE FIRST-BORN	מַכַּת בְּכֹרוֹת:

Rabbi Judah used to refer to the ten plagues by their Hebrew initials—

רַבִּי יְהוּדָה הָיָה נוֹתֵן בָּהֶם סִמָּנִים:

Spill three drops of wine:

דְּצַ"ךְ עַדַ"שׁ בְּאַחַ"ב:

DE-TZAKH   ADASH   BE-AḤAV

רַבִּי׳ יוֹסֵי הַגְּלִילִי אוֹמֵר: מִנַּיִן אַתָּה אוֹמֵר שֶׁלָּקוּ הַמִּצְרִים בְּמִצְרַיִם עֶשֶׂר
מַכּוֹת וְעַל הַיָּם לָקוּ חֲמִשִּׁים מַכּוֹת . . .

The purpose of the exchange among the three Sages concerning the number of plagues the Egyptians were afflicted with at the Red Sea is to magnify the miraculous nature of the Red Sea crossing. Each one tries to outdo the other in describing the greatness of the event. Miracle is added to miracle. This "controversy" is similar to the kind that one may hear after a particularly impressive victory when miracles are perceived to have occurred—such as happened in the Six-Day War. Soldiers and veterans regaled each other with descriptions of the battles and the supernatural aspects of the war, each storyteller trying to "top" the ones who preceded him.

There may be a deeper meaning to this midrashic passage. The Sages are telling us that the miracle at the Red Sea was of greater significance than the Egyptian plagues. From the biblical account of the parting of the Red Sea, one might have been able to conclude that the parting of the waters can be explained naturally. "And Moses stretched out his hand over the sea; and the Lord caused the sea to go back by a strong east wind all that night, and He made the sea dry land, and the waters were divided" (Ex. 14:21). There are, and always were, skeptics and cynics in the ranks of our people. At the very time that Moses hailed the Almighty with the "Song of the Sea," some of them must have been saying, "Almighty? Miracle? Nonsense! High tide, low tide!" The Torah is not perturbed by these claims. Indeed it does not insist that miracles must come from outside of nature. To be sure, the greatest miracles are found within nature. Nature is the handmaiden of the Almighty, performing His Divine will in the course of human events.

The parting of the Red Sea became the prototype of all miracles not because it contained greater supernatural qualities than other miracles, but because it had a greater impact on Jewish faith than other miracles did. The importance of a miracle is measured by its association to the Divine will that caused it. The plagues too could be explained in some scientific way, but what is crucial is that the Jews who looked at the ten plagues, and especially at the parting of the Red Sea, interpreted these events as the hand of God. After the parting of the sea, the Bible testifies, "They believed in God and in

Moses, His servant" (Ex. 14:31). This made the parting of the sea the great miracle it was.

Our generation has also witnessed great victories, even miraculous ones, against overwhelming odds—in the War of Independence, the Six-Day War, and the Yom Kippur War. We are seeing Jews returning to their homeland after two thousand years of exile, and we rejoice that Jerusalem our Holy City is united again. But these wondrous events can be considered miraculous only if we recognize them as such and are thus brought closer to the Maker of all miracles.

Rabbi Jose the Galilean said: How can one show that following the ten plagues in Egypt proper the Egyptians were smitten with fifty plagues at the Red Sea? Of one of the plagues in Egypt it is said, "The soothsayer said to Pharaoh, the plague is the finger of the might of God," while at the Red Sea it is said, "And Israel saw the strong hand which the Eternal had shown against Egypt, and the people revered the Eternal and believed in the Eternal and His servant Moses." If one finger of God in Egypt caused ten plagues, we may assume that the whole hand of God at the Red Sea caused fifty plagues.

רַבִּי יוֹסֵי הַגְּלִילִי אוֹמֵר: מִנַּיִן אַתָּה אוֹמֵר, שֶׁלָּקוּ הַמִּצְרִים בְּמִצְרַיִם עֶשֶׂר מַכּוֹת, וְעַל־הַיָּם, לָקוּ חֲמִשִּׁים מַכּוֹת. בְּמִצְרַיִם מָה הוּא אוֹמֵר: וַיֹּאמְרוּ הַחַרְטֻמִּם אֶל־פַּרְעֹה, אֶצְבַּע אֱלֹהִים הוּא. וְעַל־הַיָּם מָה הוּא אוֹמֵר: וַיַּרְא יִשְׂרָאֵל אֶת־הַיָּד הַגְּדֹלָה, אֲשֶׁר עָשָׂה יְיָ בְּמִצְרַיִם, וַיִּירְאוּ הָעָם אֶת־יְיָ. וַיַּאֲמִינוּ בַּייָ, וּבְמֹשֶׁה עַבְדּוֹ: כַּמָּה לָקוּ בְאֶצְבַּע, עֶשֶׂר מַכּוֹת. אֱמוֹר מֵעַתָּה: בְּמִצְרַיִם, לָקוּ עֶשֶׂר מַכּוֹת, וְעַל־הַיָּם, לָקוּ חֲמִשִּׁים מַכּוֹת:

Rabbi Eliezer said: How can one show that every plague which the Holy One, blessed be He, brought in Egypt upon the Egyptians was fourfold in character? For it is said: "He

רַבִּי אֱלִיעֶזֶר אוֹמֵר: מִנַּיִן שֶׁכָּל־מַכָּה וּמַכָּה, שֶׁהֵבִיא הַקָּדוֹשׁ בָּרוּךְ הוּא עַל־הַמִּצְרִים בְּמִצְרַיִם, הָיְתָה שֶׁל אַרְבַּע מַכּוֹת שֶׁנֶּאֱמַר: יְשַׁלַּח־

sent against the Egyptians in His burning anger, Wrath, Indignation, Trouble, and the Messengers of Evil." This is to be interpreted that each plague descended with Wrath (1), Indignation (2), Trouble (3), and the sending of Messengers of Evil (4). If, then, the Egyptians in Egypt were stricken with ten fourfold plagues, making forty, then following the earlier interpretation, at the Red Sea they suffered two hundred.

בָּם חֲרוֹן אַפּוֹ, עֶבְרָה וָזַעַם וְצָרָה. מִשְׁלַחַת מַלְאֲכֵי רָעִים. עֶבְרָה אַחַת. וָזַעַם שְׁתַּיִם. וְצָרָה שָׁלֹשׁ. מִשְׁלַחַת מַלְאֲכֵי רָעִים אַרְבַּע. אֱמוֹר מֵעַתָּה: בְּמִצְרַיִם, לָקוּ אַרְבָּעִים מַכּוֹת, וְעַל־הַיָּם, לָקוּ מָאתַיִם מַכּוֹת:

Rabbi Akiba said: In similar fashion you can show that every plague which the Holy One, blessed be He, brought in Egypt upon the Egyptians was fivefold in character. Interpret the same verse to say, "He sent against the Egyptians His Burning Anger (1), Wrath (2), Indignation (3), Trouble (4), and the Messengers of Evil (5)." Thus, if the Egyptians in Egypt were stricken with ten fivefold plagues, making fifty, then at the Red Sea they suffered two hundred and fifty plagues.

רַבִּי עֲקִיבָא אוֹמֵר: מִנַּיִן שֶׁכָּל־ מַכָּה וּמַכָּה שֶׁהֵבִיא הַקָּדוֹשׁ בָּרוּךְ הוּא עַל־הַמִּצְרִים בְּמִצְרַיִם, הָיְתָה שֶׁל חָמֵשׁ מַכּוֹת. שֶׁנֶּאֱמַר: יְשַׁלַּח־ בָּם חֲרוֹן אַפּוֹ עֶבְרָה וָזַעַם וְצָרָה מִשְׁלַחַת מַלְאֲכֵי רָעִים. חֲרוֹן אַפּוֹ אַחַת. עֶבְרָה שְׁתַּיִם. וָזַעַם שָׁלֹשׁ. וְצָרָה אַרְבַּע. מִשְׁלַחַת מַלְאֲכֵי רָעִים חָמֵשׁ. אֱמוֹר מֵעַתָּה: בְּמִצְרַיִם, לָקוּ חֲמִשִּׁים מַכּוֹת, וְעַל הַיָּם, לָקוּ חֲמִשִּׁים וּמָאתַיִם מַכּוֹת:

אֵלּוּ הוֹצִיאָנוּ

דַּיֵּנוּ

The essential message of דַּיֵּנוּ is *hakorat hatov*—expression of gratitude for someone's beneficence. In this case we express our thankfulness to God for a whole series of events whereby He showed us favor.

Hakorat hatov does not always come easy. It is usually easier to complain about what we are lacking than to rejoice over what we have. The best model of gratitude in biblical history is that of Jacob, who at the end of his life blessed his grandchildren, Manasseh and Ephraim, with "May the Almighty God who has been my shepherd from birth to this day—may the angel who has redeemed me from all evil bless these children" (Gen. 48:15–16). Jacob is the last person we would expect to be so effusive in his gratitude for a good life. The life of our forefather was filled with tragedy: he was in a constant struggle with his brother, Esau, and even had to flee the country to escape with his life; the next phase of his life was filled with conflict with his deceptive father-in-law, Laban; and his return to Canaan brought the loss of his beloved Rachel. Later he suffered shame and embarrassment from Dinah's affair with Shechem and the subsequent revenge wrought by Simeon and Levi. As if this were not enough, his favorite, Joseph, was snatched from him and for over twenty years was thought to be dead. Even after they were reunited, it had to be in exile, away from Jacob's birthplace in the Land of Israel. Yet in spite of all of these difficulties and misfortunes, Jacob is still able at the end of his life to express gratitude for the strength and the Divine guidance that enabled him to overcome all the tragedies of his life. Not a word of complaint! If we could only learn to accept fully the joys of life, to be happy and grateful for what we have, and to be satisfied with less, how much fuller and more gratifying our lives would be.

כַּמָּה מַעֲלוֹת טוֹבוֹת לַמָּקוֹם עָלֵינוּ:

אֵלּוּ הוֹצִיאָנוּ מִמִּצְרַיִם,
וְלֹא־עָשָׂה בָהֶם שְׁפָטִים,
דַּיֵּנוּ:

אִלּוּ קֵרְבָנוּ לִפְנֵי הַר סִינַי וְלֹא נָתַן לָנוּ אֶת הַתּוֹרָה

אִלּוּ קֵרְבָנוּ לִפְנֵי הַר סִינַי וְלֹא נָתַן לָנוּ אֶת הַתּוֹרָה is especially troublesome.
It is easy to understand that had the Almighty just taken us out of
Egypt and not brought us to Sinai, it would have been sufficient.
But what would we have gained from standing at Mount Sinai
without receiving the Torah? The answer is that standing at Mount
Sinai enabled us to feel and experience the Divine Presence. During
this time we prepared for the Divine encounter. We separated ourselves from our spouses in order to purify our bodies. Undoubtedly
we cleansed our minds of impure thoughts. The very preparation
itself with its sense of Divine nearness and protection would have
been sufficient! But the Almighty did even more for us; not only
did He enable us to feel His presence, but in an act of kindness and
compassion, He revealed to us His Divine will in His Torah in order
to teach us how to live. And so we thank God on Passover night for
bringing us close to Mount Sinai and granting us His Torah by
whose laws we conduct this beautiful Passover Seder each year.

It should be noted that there are other occasions in which we
perceive the preparation for a mitzvah or an event to be of equal, if
not greater, importance than the final objective. It is during the
preparatory period that one is fully occupied with the mitzvah that
is to take place. To use an analogy, the cooking takes longer than
the eating. Hasidim especially recognize this concept and will often
spend more time preparing for their prayers than actually praying.
To them, to give another example, the four-day period before
Sukkot, during which time the *sukkah* is being built and the *lulav*
purchased, is greater even than the succeeding days of the festival.

How thankful must we be to God, the All-Present, for all the
good He did for us.

Had He brought us out from Egypt

And not executed judgment against them,

It would have been enough for us!

אִלּוּ עָשָׂה בָהֶם שְׁפָטִים,
וְלֹא־עָשָׂה בֵאלֹהֵיהֶם,
דַּיֵּנוּ.

אִלּוּ עָשָׂה בֵאלֹהֵיהֶם,
וְלֹא־הָרַג אֶת־בְּכוֹרֵיהֶם,
דַּיֵּנוּ:

אִלּוּ הָרַג אֶת־בְּכוֹרֵיהֶם,
וְלֹא־נָתַן לָנוּ אֶת־מָמוֹנָם,
דַּיֵּנוּ:

אִלּוּ נָתַן לָנוּ אֶת־מָמוֹנָם,
וְלֹא־קָרַע לָנוּ אֶת־הַיָּם,
דַּיֵּנוּ:

אִלּוּ קָרַע לָנוּ אֶת־הַיָּם,
וְלֹא־הֶעֱבִירָנוּ בְתוֹכוֹ בֶּחָרָבָה,
דַּיֵּנוּ:

אִלּוּ הֶעֱבִירָנוּ בְתוֹכוֹ בֶּחָרָבָה,
וְלֹא־שִׁקַּע צָרֵינוּ בְּתוֹכוֹ,
דַּיֵּנוּ:

אִלּוּ שִׁקַּע צָרֵינוּ בְּתוֹכוֹ,
וְלֹא־סִפֵּק צָרְכֵּנוּ בַּמִּדְבָּר אַרְבָּעִים שָׁנָה,
דַּיֵּנוּ:

אִלּוּ סִפֵּק צָרְכֵּנוּ בַּמִּדְבָּר אַרְבָּעִים שָׁנָה,
וְלֹא־הֶאֱכִילָנוּ אֶת־הַמָּן,
דַּיֵּנוּ:

Had He executed judgment against them
  And not executed [judgment] against their idols,
   It would have been enough for us!

Had He executed [judgment] against their idols
  And not slain their first-born,
   It would have been enough for us!

Had He slain their first-born
  And not given us their property,
   It would have been enough for us!

Had He given us their property,
  And not divided the sea for us,
   It would have been enough for us!

Had He divided the sea for us
  And not brought us through it dry-shod,
   It would have been enough for us!

Had He brought us through it dry-shod
  And not drowned our oppressors in it,
   It would have been enough for us!

Had He drowned our oppressors in it
  And not helped us for forty years in the desert,
   It would have been enough for us!

Had He helped us for forty years in the desert
  And not fed us manna,
   It would have been enough for us!

אִלּוּ הֶאֱכִילָנוּ אֶת־הַמָּן,
וְלֹא־נָתַן לָנוּ אֶת־הַשַּׁבָּת,
דַּיֵּנוּ:

אִלּוּ נָתַן לָנוּ אֶת הַשַּׁבָּת,
וְלֹא קֵרְבָנוּ לִפְנֵי הַר־סִינַי,
דַּיֵּנוּ:

אִלּוּ קֵרְבָנוּ לִפְנֵי הַר־סִינַי,
וְלֹא־נָתַן לָנוּ אֶת־הַתּוֹרָה,
דַּיֵּנוּ:

אִלּוּ נָתַן לָנוּ אֶת־הַתּוֹרָה,
וְלֹא־הִכְנִיסָנוּ לְאֶרֶץ יִשְׂרָאֵל,
דַּיֵּנוּ:

אִלּוּ הִכְנִיסָנוּ לְאֶרֶץ יִשְׂרָאֵל,
וְלֹא־בָנָה לָנוּ אֶת־בֵּית הַבְּחִירָה,
דַּיֵּנוּ:

עַל אַחַת כַּמָּה וְכַמָּה, טוֹבָה כְפוּלָה וּמְכֻפֶּלֶת, לַמָּקוֹם עָלֵינוּ.

שֶׁהוֹצִיאָנוּ מִמִּצְרַיִם,
וְעָשָׂה בָהֶם שְׁפָטִים,
וְעָשָׂה בֵאלֹהֵיהֶם,
וְהָרַג אֶת־בְּכוֹרֵיהֶם,
וְנָתַן לָנוּ אֶת־מָמוֹנָם,
וְקָרַע לָנוּ אֶת־הַיָּם,
וְהֶעֱבִירָנוּ בְתוֹכוֹ בֶּחָרָבָה,
וְשִׁקַּע צָרֵינוּ בְּתוֹכוֹ,

Had He fed us manna

    And not given us the Sabbath,

        It would have been enough for us!

Had He given us the Sabbath

    And not brought us to Mount Sinai,

        It would have been enough for us!

Had He brought us to Mount Sinai

    And not given us the Torah,

        It would have been enough for us!

Had He given us the Torah

    And not brought us into the Land of Israel,

        It would have been enough for us!

Had He brought us to the Land of Israel

    And not built for us the Holy Temple,

        It would have been enough for us!

How much more so do we have to be thankful for the manifold
and unbounded blessings of the All-Present God:

That He brought us out from Egypt,

    And executed judgment against them,

And executed [judgment] against their idols,

    And slew their first-born,

And gave us their property,

    And divided the sea for us,

And brought us through it dry-shod,

    And drowned our oppressors in it,

וְסִפֵּק צָרְכֵּנוּ בַּמִּדְבָּר אַרְבָּעִים שָׁנָה,

וְהֶאֱכִילָנוּ אֶת־הַמָּן,

וְנָתַן לָנוּ אֶת־הַשַּׁבָּת,

וְקֵרְבָנוּ לִפְנֵי הַר־סִינַי,

וְנָתַן לָנוּ אֶת־הַתּוֹרָה,

וְהִכְנִיסָנוּ לְאֶרֶץ יִשְׂרָאֵל,

וּבָנָה לָנוּ אֶת־בֵּית הַבְּחִירָה

לְכַפֵּר עַל־כָּל־עֲוֹנוֹתֵינוּ.

Rabban Gamliel used to say: Whoever does not explain the following three symbols at the Seder on Passover has not fulfilled his duty:	רַבָּן גַּמְלִיאֵל הָיָה אוֹמֵר: כָּל שֶׁלֹּא אָמַר שְׁלֹשָׁה דְבָרִים אֵלּוּ בַּפֶּסַח, לֹא יָצָא יְדֵי חוֹבָתוֹ. וְאֵלּוּ הֵן:

THE PASSOVER OFFERING	פֶּסַח.
THE MATZAH	מַצָּה.
THE BITTER HERBS	וּמָרוֹר:

פֶּסַח . . . עַל שׁוּם מָה? עַל שׁוּם שֶׁפָּסַח הַקָּבָּ״ה עַל בָּתֵּי אֲבוֹתֵנוּ בְּמִצְרַיִם

Targum Onkelos translates the Hebrew term פֶּסַח not as "passing over" but as "having mercy" (Exodus 12:13). Passover is the festival par excellence that commemorates God's love and mercy for the Jewish people. Despite their assimilation, despite the fact that the Hebrews had forgotten their heritage, despite their attempts to become more Egyptian than the Egyptians, God nevertheless demonstrated His love for Israel—by passing over the Jewish homes and striking only at the Egyptians.

The *korban pesah* is our demonstration of love for the Almighty. The Israelites were willing to put their lives on the line and sacrifice an animal that the Egyptians venerated, because God had stepped into history to redeem them although they were not yet worthy of redemption.

And helped us for forty years in the desert,

And fed us manna,

And gave us the Sabbath,

And brought us to Mount Sinai,

And gave us the Torah,

And brought us into the Land of Israel,

And built for us the Holy Temple

Where we could atone for all our sins.

The Passover offering which our fathers ate in Temple days, what was the reason for it? It was because the Holy One, blessed be He, passed over the houses of our forefathers in Egypt, as it is written in the Bible: "And you shall say it is the Passover offering for the Eternal, Who passed over the houses of the children of Israel in Egypt when He smote the Egyptians and spared our houses. And the people bowed their heads and worshipped."

פֶּסַח שֶׁהָיוּ אֲבוֹתֵינוּ אוֹכְלִים, בִּזְמַן שֶׁבֵּית־הַמִּקְדָּשׁ הָיָה קַיָּם, עַל־שׁוּם מָה? עַל־שׁוּם, שֶׁפָּסַח הַקָּדוֹשׁ בָּרוּךְ הוּא, עַל־בָּתֵּי אֲבוֹתֵינוּ בְּמִצְרָיִם. שֶׁנֶּאֱמַר: וַאֲמַרְתֶּם זֶבַח־פֶּסַח הוּא לַיְיָ, אֲשֶׁר פָּסַח עַל־בָּתֵּי בְנֵי־יִשְׂרָאֵל בְּמִצְרַיִם, בְּנָגְפּוֹ אֶת־מִצְרַיִם, וְאֶת־בָּתֵּינוּ הִצִּיל. וַיִּקֹּד הָעָם וַיִּשְׁתַּחֲווּ:

מַצָּה . . . עַל שׁוּם מָה? עַל שׁוּם שֶׁלֹּא הִסְפִּיק . . .

There is more to the eating of matzah on the Exodus night than the reminder that the Jews had no time to bake bread and had to rush. God instructed the Israelites to bake matzah instead of bread to impress upon the Jews a reordering of priorities. Had they been given a chance, some would even have delayed the Exodus in order to provide themselves with more luxurious food, for to a slave the greatest enjoyment comes from a good meal. But now, leaving

Egypt with matzah instead of challah meant leaving behind the comforts of a material existence to brave the desert. There is only so much food that can be prepared in advance. With little time for food preparation, the Jews could not hold out long without the help of the Almighty. The Exodus was, therefore, a demonstration of faith, and the journey in the desert became a journey of faith. Faith begins where certainty of material support is lacking.

As we noted earlier, matzah has a dual symbolism. It stands for servitude and want as the poor bread our fathers ate in Egypt, and it expresses freedom as the bread that the Jews took with them out of Egypt into the desert. The Zohar offers yet a third interpretation in line with our own theory (paragraph above). Matzah is the bread that the Jews took with them when they followed the Almighty into uncharted territory, into a place they knew not. The Zohar labels this matzah לַחְמָא דִמְהֵימְנוּתָא—the bread of faith.

Raise the broken middle matzah and say:

This matzah which we eat, what is the reason for it? It is because there was not time for the dough of our ancestors in Egypt to become leavened, before the Ruler of all, the Holy One, blessed be He, revealed Himself to them and redeemed them, as it is told in the Bible: "And the dough which they had brought out from Egypt they baked into cakes of unleavened bread, for it had not leavened, because

מַצָּה זוֹ שֶׁאָנוּ אוֹכְלִים עַל־שׁוּם מָה? עַל־שׁוּם, שֶׁלֹּא הִסְפִּיק בְּצֵקָם שֶׁל אֲבוֹתֵינוּ לְהַחֲמִיץ, עַד שֶׁנִּגְלָה עֲלֵיהֶם, מֶלֶךְ מַלְכֵי הַמְּלָכִים הַקָּדוֹשׁ בָּרוּךְ הוּא, וּגְאָלָם. שֶׁנֶּאֱמַר: וַיֹּאפוּ אֶת־ הַבָּצֵק, אֲשֶׁר הוֹצִיאוּ מִמִּצְרַיִם, עֻגֹת מַצּוֹת כִּי לֹא חָמֵץ. כִּי־גֹרְשׁוּ מִמִּצְרַיִם, וְלֹא יָכְלוּ לְהִתְמַהְמֵהַּ, וְגַם־צֵדָה לֹא־עָשׂוּ לָהֶם:

they were thrust out of Egypt and they could not tarry, nor had they prepared for themselves any provisions."

Raise the bitter herbs:

These bitter herbs which we eat, what is their meaning? They are eaten to recall that

מָרוֹר זֶה שֶׁאָנוּ אוֹכְלִים עַל־שׁוּם מָה? עַל־שׁוּם, שֶׁמֵּרְרוּ הַמִּצְרִים

the Egyptians embittered the lives of our forefathers in Egypt, as it is written: "And they embittered their lives with hard labor: with mortar and bricks, with every kind of work in the fields; all the work which they made them do was hard labor."

אֶת־חַיֵּי אֲבוֹתֵינוּ בְּמִצְרַיִם, שֶׁנֶּאֱמַר: וַיְמָרְרוּ אֶת־חַיֵּיהֶם בַּעֲבֹדָה קָשָׁה, בְּחֹמֶר וּבִלְבֵנִים, וּבְכָל־עֲבֹדָה בַּשָּׂדֶה. אֵת כָּל־עֲבֹדָתָם, אֲשֶׁר־עָבְדוּ בָהֶם בְּפָרֶךְ׃

בְּכָל דּוֹר וָדוֹר חַיָּב אָדָם לִרְאוֹת אֶת עַצְמוֹ כְּאִלּוּ הוּא יָצָא מִמִּצְרַיִם

Instead of לִרְאוֹת אֶת עַצְמוֹ, Maimonides' Haggadah reads לְהַרְאוֹת אֶת עַצְמוֹ—one is obligated "to show" or "to portray" himself as if he left Egypt. This reading is in accord with the notion that in every act there should be an external moment and an internal moment that are in harmony. These are called respectively מַעֲשֵׂה הַמִּצְוָה, the performance, and כַּוָּנַת הַמִּצְוָה, the inward emotional content of the action. How can one generate the proper inner feelings? There is an inseparable bond between what we do and what we are, and between what we do and what we think. By acting and portraying ourselves as if we lived in Egypt and left during the Exodus, we actually think of ourselves that way. Inwardly we will feel the story of slavery and redemption. This does not represent hypocritical action. A hypocrite pretends to be what he is not. A truly religious person thinks and does in order to become what he believes he ought to be.

From this perspective we can appreciate the story of the man who was concerned with the problem of "the righteous who suffer and the wicked who prosper" and asked his local rav for an answer to this agonizing question. The rav, confessing himself unable to deal with so profound a question, suggested that the man go to Haniopoli and ask the great Rabbi Zusya. In Haniopoli the man was told that he would find Rabbi Zusya in a corner of the study house. When he entered the *beit hamidrash*, he saw an emaciated man with pale, yellowing skin, dressed in tattered clothing. He turned to him. "Are you the renowned Rabbi Zusya?" "I am Zusya," came the reply. "I want to ask you about the suffering of the righteous, but apparently you are suffering. So how can I ask you such a question?" "I suffering?" answered Rabbi Zusya. "I am the most blessed of human beings. I sit here in the study house, protected by the Almighty. Whatever physical needs I may have are met. I can study His holy Torah. I don't suffer at all." With tears in his eyes, the Jew left. His question had been answered. Suffering is in the eyes of the sufferer. If one acts and thinks and feels near to the Almighty, one is redeemed.

In every generation one must look upon himself as if he personally had come out from Egypt, as the Bible says: "And thou shalt tell thy son on that day, saying, it is because of that which the Eternal did to me when I went forth from Egypt." For it was not our forefathers alone whom the Holy One, blessed be He, redeemed; He redeemed us too, with them, as it is said: "He brought us out from there that He might lead us to and give us the land which He pledged to our forefathers."

בְּכָל־דּוֹר וָדוֹר חַיָּב אָדָם לִרְאוֹת אֶת־עַצְמוֹ, כְּאִלּוּ הוּא יָצָא מִמִּצְרַיִם. שֶׁנֶּאֱמַר: וְהִגַּדְתָּ לְבִנְךָ בַּיּוֹם הַהוּא לֵאמֹר. בַּעֲבוּר זֶה, עָשָׂה יְיָ לִי, בְּצֵאתִי מִמִּצְרַיִם: לֹא אֶת־אֲבוֹתֵינוּ בִּלְבָד גָּאַל הַקָּדוֹשׁ בָּרוּךְ הוּא, אֶלָּא אַף אוֹתָנוּ גָּאַל עִמָּהֶם. שֶׁנֶּאֱמַר: וְאוֹתָנוּ הוֹצִיא מִשָּׁם. לְמַעַן הָבִיא אֹתָנוּ, לָתֶת לָנוּ אֶת־הָאָרֶץ, אֲשֶׁר נִשְׁבַּע לַאֲבֹתֵינוּ:

Cover the matzot, raise the cup of wine, and say:

Therefore, it is our duty to thank and to praise in song and prayer, to glorify and extol Him Who performed all these wonders for our forefathers and for us. He brought us out from slavery to freedom, from anguish to joy, from sorrow to festivity, from darkness to great light. Let us therefore sing before Him a new song. Praise the Eternal.

לְפִיכָךְ, אֲנַחְנוּ חַיָּבִים לְהוֹדוֹת, לְהַלֵּל, לְשַׁבֵּחַ, לְפָאֵר, לְרוֹמֵם, לְהַדֵּר, לְבָרֵךְ, לְעַלֵּה וּלְקַלֵּס, לְמִי שֶׁעָשָׂה לַאֲבוֹתֵינוּ וְלָנוּ, אֶת־כָּל־ הַנִּסִּים הָאֵלּוּ. הוֹצִיאָנוּ מֵעַבְדוּת לְחֵרוּת. מִיָּגוֹן לְשִׂמְחָה. וּמֵאֵבֶל לְיוֹם טוֹב. וּמֵאֲפֵלָה לְאוֹר גָּדוֹל. וּמִשִּׁעְבּוּד לִגְאֻלָּה. וְנֹאמַר לְפָנָיו שִׁירָה חֲדָשָׁה, הַלְלוּיָהּ:

Put down the cup and continue:

הַלְלוּיָה . . .

Hallel is recited at the Seder in accordance with the halakhah that we utter this thanksgiving prayer whenever the Almighty has saved us from misfortune. The *Hallel* at the Seder is unusual in two respects. First, it is not preceded by a blessing as it is on festival days, when we recite *Hallel* in the morning. Second, it is divided into two parts, separated by the meal. The first section, known as הַלֵּל הַמִּצְרִי—the Egyptian *Hallel*, deals specifically with the redemption from Egypt. The second section praises the Almighty for the ultimate redemption of the Jewish people and the world.

Why do we not recite the blessing for *Hallel* on this night of thanksgiving? The answer lies in the unique nature of the Seder. Ordinarily when we recite *Hallel*, we do so either because it is a festival or a commemoration of an event in the past. Neither applies to the *Hallel* of the Seder.° At the Passover Seder we do not celebrate an event of the distant past, for we ourselves were saved and redeemed from Egypt. The thanksgiving psalm is then a natural outpouring of gratitude to God. For this kind of natural reaction, a blessing is not recited.

° While the night of the fifteenth of Nisan is a holiday, the *Hallel* is not recited then in the capacity of a festival *Hallel*, for the *Hallel* we recite in the morning fulfills that role.

הַלְלוּיָהּ.

הַלְלוּ עַבְדֵי יְיָ. הַלְלוּ אֶת־שֵׁם יְיָ:

יְהִי שֵׁם יְיָ מְבֹרָךְ. מֵעַתָּה וְעַד־עוֹלָם:

מִמִּזְרַח־שֶׁמֶשׁ עַד־מְבוֹאוֹ. מְהֻלָּל שֵׁם יְיָ:

רָם עַל־כָּל־גּוֹיִם יְיָ. עַל הַשָּׁמַיִם כְּבוֹדוֹ:

מִי כַּיְיָ אֱלֹהֵינוּ. הַמַּגְבִּיהִי לָשָׁבֶת:

הַמַּשְׁפִּילִי לִרְאוֹת בַּשָּׁמַיִם וּבָאָרֶץ:

מְקִימִי מֵעָפָר דָּל, מֵאַשְׁפֹּת יָרִים אֶבְיוֹן:

לְהוֹשִׁיבִי עִם־נְדִיבִים עִם נְדִיבֵי עַמּוֹ:

מוֹשִׁיבִי עֲקֶרֶת הַבַּיִת אֵם־הַבָּנִים שְׂמֵחָה, הַלְלוּיָהּ:

בְּצֵאת יִשְׂרָאֵל מִמִּצְרָיִם. בֵּית יַעֲקֹב מֵעַם לֹעֵז:

הָיְתָה יְהוּדָה לְקָדְשׁוֹ. יִשְׂרָאֵל מַמְשְׁלוֹתָיו:

הַיָּם רָאָה וַיָּנֹס. הַיַּרְדֵּן יִסֹּב לְאָחוֹר:

הֶהָרִים רָקְדוּ כְאֵילִים. גְּבָעוֹת כִּבְנֵי־צֹאן:

מַה־לְּךָ הַיָּם כִּי תָנוּס. הַיַּרְדֵּן תִּסֹּב לְאָחוֹר:

הֶהָרִים תִּרְקְדוּ כְאֵילִים. גְּבָעוֹת כִּבְנֵי־צֹאן:

מִלִּפְנֵי אָדוֹן חוּלִי אָרֶץ. מִלִּפְנֵי אֱלוֹהַּ יַעֲקֹב:

הַהֹפְכִי הַצּוּר אֲגַם־מָיִם. חַלָּמִישׁ לְמַעְיְנוֹ־מָיִם:

Halleluyah—Praise the Eternal.
Praise, ye servants of the Eternal,
  Praise the name of the Eternal.
Blessed be the name of the Eternal
  From now and for evermore:
From the rising of the sun to its going down.
  Praised be the name of the Eternal.
Supreme above all the nations is the Eternal:
  His glory is above the heavens.
Who is like unto the Eternal our God,
  Throned in exaltation,
Who looks down
  to both the heavens and the earth?
He raises up the poor from the dust,
  Lifts up the needy from the ash-heap,
To seat them with princes,
  With princes of His people;
He makes the childless woman dwell in her household
  As a joyful mother of children.
Halleluyah—Praise the Eternal.

When Israel went forth from Egypt,
  The house of Jacob from a people of strange tongue,
Judah became His sanctuary, Israel His dominion.
  The sea beheld and fled, The Jordan turned back.
The mountains skipped like rams, The hills like lambs.
  What ails thee, O sea, that thou didst flee,
Jordan, that thou turnest back,
  You mountains, that you skip like rams, You hills, like lambs?
Tremble, thou earth, at the presence of the Eternal,
  At the presence of the God of Jacob,
Who turns the rock into a pool of water,
  The flint into a fountain of water.

בא״י . . . אֲשֶׁר גְּאָלָנוּ וְגָאַל אֶת אֲבוֹתֵינוּ . . .

In the concluding blessing of *maggid,* in which we give special thanks to the Almighty, who has redeemed us and redeemed our fathers from Egypt, our redemption is mentioned first, for by this time we have completely identified with our fathers. As is natural, one rejoices more over his own redemption.

On Passover night we not only look backward, but we also look to the future. We thus conclude with the prayer, ''Just as we have been brought to this day . . .'' The theme of future redemption will be taken up after the meal in the second part of the *Hallel.*

Raise the cup of wine and say:

Blessed art Thou, Eternal our God, Ruler of the universe, Who redeemed us and redeemed our forefathers from Egypt, and brought us to this night to eat thereon matzah and bitter herbs. Thus may the Eternal our God and God of our fathers bring us to future feasts and festivals in peace; and to the upbuilding of Your city Jerusalem, and to the happiness of Your service, so that we may partake there of the ancient offerings. We shall then offer unto You a new song for our redemption and salvation. Blessed art Thou, Eternal, Who redeemed Israel.

בָּרוּךְ אַתָּה יְיָ, אֱלֹהֵינוּ מֶלֶךְ הָעוֹלָם, אֲשֶׁר גְּאָלָנוּ וְגָאַל אֶת־ אֲבוֹתֵינוּ מִמִּצְרַיִם, וְהִגִּיעָנוּ הַלַּיְלָה הַזֶּה, לֶאֱכָל־בּוֹ מַצָּה וּמָרוֹר. כֵּן, יְיָ אֱלֹהֵינוּ וֵאלֹהֵי אֲבוֹתֵינוּ, יַגִּיעֵנוּ לְמוֹעֲדִים וְלִרְגָלִים אֲחֵרִים, הַבָּאִים לִקְרָאתֵנוּ לְשָׁלוֹם, שְׂמֵחִים בְּבִנְיַן עִירֶךָ, וְשָׂשִׂים בַּעֲבוֹדָתֶךָ, וְנֹאכַל שָׁם מִן הַזְּבָחִים וּמִן הַפְּסָחִים (במוצאי שבת אומרים מִן הַפְּסָחִים וּמִן הַזְּבָחִים), אֲשֶׁר יַגִּיעַ דָּמָם, עַל־ קִיר מִזְבַּחֲךָ לְרָצוֹן, וְנוֹדֶה לְךָ שִׁיר חָדָשׁ עַל־גְּאֻלָּתֵנוּ, וְעַל־פְּדוּת נַפְשֵׁנוּ: בָּרוּךְ אַתָּה יְיָ, גָּאַל יִשְׂרָאֵל:

THE SECOND CUP

כּוֹס שְׁנִיָּה

הִנְנִי מוּכָן וּמְזֻמָּן לְקַיֵּם מִצְוַת כּוֹס שְׁנִיָּה מֵאַרְבַּע כּוֹסוֹת לְשֵׁם יִחוּד קוּדְשָׁא בְּרִיךְ־הוּא וּשְׁכִינְתֵּיהּ עַל־יְדֵי הַהוּא טָמִיר וְנֶעְלָם בְּשֵׁם כָּל־יִשְׂרָאֵל.

Blessed art Thou, Eternal our God, Ruler of the universe, Creator of the fruit of the vine.

בָּרוּךְ אַתָּה יְיָ, אֱלֹהֵינוּ מֶלֶךְ הָעוֹלָם, בּוֹרֵא פְּרִי הַגָּפֶן:

Drink the second cup of wine while leaning to the left.

RAHTZAH

רָחְצָה

WASHING THE HANDS

A large cup of water is brought to the table. It is poured twice over the right hand and twice over the left hand. The blessing is recited and the hands are dried.

Blessed art Thou, Eternal our God, Ruler of the universe, Who made us holy with His commandments, and com- manded us concerning the washing of the hands.

בָּרוּךְ אַתָּה יְיָ, אֱלֹהֵינוּ מֶלֶךְ הָעוֹלָם, אֲשֶׁר קִדְּשָׁנוּ בְּמִצְוֹתָיו, וְצִוָּנוּ עַל־נְטִילַת יָדָיִם:

MOTZI AND MATZAH   מוֹצִיא מַצָּה

EATING THE MATZAH

הִנְנִי מוּכָן וּמְזֻמָּן לְקַיֵּם מִצְוַת אֲכִילַת מַצָּה, לְשֵׁם יִחוּד קוּדְשָׁא בְּרִיךְ־הוּא
וּשְׁכִינְתֵּיה עַל־יְדֵי הַהוּא טָמִיר וְנֶעְלָם בְּשֵׁם כָּל־יִשְׂרָאֵל.

Say the first blessing while holding all three matzot.

Blessed art Thou, Eternal our God, Ruler of the universe, Who brings forth bread from the earth.

בָּרוּךְ אַתָּה יְיָ, אֱלֹהֵינוּ מֶלֶךְ
הָעוֹלָם, הַמּוֹצִיא לֶחֶם מִן־הָאָרֶץ:

*Say the second blessing while holding only the top
and broken middle matzot.*

Blessed art Thou, Eternal our God, Ruler of the universe, Who made us holy with His commandments, and commanded us concerning the eating of matzah.

בָּרוּךְ אַתָּה יְיָ, אֱלֹהֵינוּ מֶלֶךְ
הָעוֹלָם, אֲשֶׁר קִדְּשָׁנוּ בְּמִצְוֹתָיו,
וְצִוָּנוּ עַל־אֲכִילַת מַצָּה:

Eat of the top and broken middle matzot.

MAROR

מָרוֹר

BITTER HERBS

הִנְנִי מוּכָן וּמְזֻמָּן לְקַיֵּם מִצְוַת אֲכִילַת מָרוֹר, לְשֵׁם יִחוּד קוּדְשָׁא בְּרִיךְ הוּא
וּשְׁכִינְתֵּיהּ עַל יְדֵי הַהוּא טָמִיר וְנֶעְלָם בְּשֵׁם כָּל־יִשְׂרָאֵל:

Dip bitter herbs in ḥaroset and say:

Blessed art Thou, Eternal our God, Ruler of the universe, Who made us holy with His commandments, and commanded us concerning the eating of bitter herbs.

בָּרוּךְ אַתָּה יְיָ, אֱלֹהֵינוּ מֶלֶךְ
הָעוֹלָם, אֲשֶׁר קִדְּשָׁנוּ בְּמִצְוֹתָיו,
וְצִוָּנוּ עַל־אֲכִילַת מָרוֹר:

Eat the bitter herbs.

KOREKH

כּוֹרֵךְ

EATING THE BITTER HERBS AND MATZAH TOGETHER

Eat a sandwich of bitter herbs and the bottom matzah and say:

In remembrance of the holy Temple, we do as Hillel did in Temple times: he put matzah and bitter herbs together and ate them as a sandwich, in order to observe literally the words of the Torah: "They shall eat it (the Passover offering) with matzah and bitter herbs."

זֵכֶר לְמִקְדָּשׁ כְּהִלֵּל. כֵּן עָשָׂה הִלֵּל,
בִּזְמַן שֶׁבֵּית הַמִּקְדָּשׁ הָיָה קַיָּם.
הָיָה כּוֹרֵךְ מַצָּה וּמָרוֹר וְאוֹכֵל
בְּיַחַד. לְקַיֵּם מַה שֶּׁנֶּאֱמַר: עַל־
מַצּוֹת וּמְרֹרִים יֹאכְלֻהוּ:

SHULḤAN OREKH

שֻׁלְחָן עוֹרֵךְ

THE FESTIVAL MEAL

THE MEANING OF AFIKOMAN

צָפוּן

The portion of matzah that we eat at the end of the meal—after which we eat nothing else—is called *afikoman*. The exact meaning of this word is not certain. It comes from the Mishnah, which states briefly: אֵין מַפְטִירִין אַחַר הַפֶּסַח אֲפִיקוֹמָן "One does not have *afikoman* after the paschal meal" (*Pesaḥim* 10:8). The Rabbis themselves split over the meaning of the term. Most held—and this is the view we commonly accept—that *afikoman* refers to dessert. In Temple times the "dessert" was the paschal lamb. The Mishnah then exhorts us not to partake of dessert, or any kind of food, after we have eaten the sacrificial meat. The reason for this rule is to preserve the taste of the *korban* in our mouths and thereby show our love for the mitzvah and our desire to cling to it. Nowadays, with no paschal sacrifices, the Talmud substitutes matzah for the paschal lamb, and we are bidden not to eat anything after the final portion of matzah that is consumed at the end of the meal.

There is one opinion in the Talmud which interprets *afikoman* differently. Rav holds that this term refers to going away from one place to another. After one has eaten the sacrificial meat, one may not go to someone else's Seder to partake of food lest one also partake of the paschal sacrifice, for it is forbidden to eat the sacrificial meat in more than one place. This regulation, expressed in Hebrew as שֶׁלֹּא יַעַקְרוּ מֵחֲבוּרָה לַחֲבוּרָה—"they shall not go from one group to another"—has great symbolic meaning. There are many people who run from house to house, so busy with others that they do not have enough time for themselves and their own kin. In effect they are escaping from their own families and shirking responsibilities that a husband and father should shoulder. On a national level there is a tendency to go to different cultures, never satisfied with one's own. Passover is the birthday of our people. It is devoted to our own national pursuits. Don't flit from house to house, from culture to culture. Tonight, at least, study your own heritage, remain with your family and in your own house. Strengthen the relationships with your own people.

Afikoman vs. Matzah
at the Beginning of the Meal

There is an obligation to eat an olive-size piece (כְּזַיִת) of matzah twice during the Seder, once when we make the blessing of עַל אֲכִילַת מַצָּה after *maggid* and a second time after the meal (the *afikoman*).° Which is the more important of the two is a matter of dispute among the Rishonim. Some consider the eating of the matzah at the beginning of the meal as the primary fulfillment of the mitzvah, since this is the matzah upon which we make a blessing. This is the opinion of the Tosafot and Rosh (R. Asher b. Yeḥiel, ca. 1250–1327). Rambam and Rif (R. Isaac Alfasi, 1013–1103), however, hold that the *afikoman* is the more important of the two portions and that the blessing of עַל אֲכִילַת מַצָּה is made earlier only because it is inappropriate to recite this blessing after we have already consumed matzah. A practical difference between these two views is the procedure to follow if one has only enough מַצָּה שְׁמוּרָה (the kind of matzah that is used at the Seder) for only one כְּזַיִת. Should he eat it before the meal or save it for the *afikoman?*

While one can explain the two divergent opinions on purely halakhic grounds, one can find a deeper, philosophic basis for the controversy. In Exodus 16 the Torah speaks of the manna—the matzah from heaven that sustained the Israelites during their difficult sojourn in the desert. The Torah regards the manna as a test "whether the people will walk in accordance with God's Torah or not" (verse 4). How did the manna test the faith of the Israelites? Ibn Ezra explains that since the manna could not be stored, for it would spoil if kept overnight, the Jews never had sufficient food for the next day. Thus, they never had a real sense of security. Who knew whether manna would fall the next day? Only faith and belief in God's kindness allowed them to have any peace of mind. Thus the manna was regarded as a kind of test of אֱמוּנָה (faith).

The *Orḥot Ḥayyim* says the opposite. He insists that the manna provided the most utopian system of plenty. There was no fear of want because the people knew each day that no matter what they did or did not do, abundant food would come raining down from

---

° This does not include the כְּזַיִת of matzah that is eaten during *Korekh* (Hillel's sandwich), for that is a *minhag* and not an obligation.

heaven. Only under such circumstances of bounty can there be a true test of faith, for when the Jew is in need, it is but natural to turn to God. When one is in the depths of despair, he has no other choice. "There are no atheists in a foxhole," as the popular saying goes. In the desert, however, when the Jews "waxed fat," they were indeed tested by the manna to see whether they maintained their faith in God as the ultimate Provider.

Bearing in mind these opposing explanations, we can explain the difference of opinion between the Tosafot and Rosh on one hand and Rif and Rambam on the other. As we mentioned above, matzah is called לַחְמָא דִמְהֵימְנוּתָא because it is a symbol of our faith. The Tosafot and Rosh find in the matzah the greatest sign of faithfulness and devotion to the Almighty. They find it in the הָא לַחְמָא עַנְיָא—"Here is the poor bread that our fathers ate in the land of Egypt." There the Jews were constantly hungry, constantly tired, constantly thirsty, and still they reached out to God. Hence the first portion of matzah must be eaten בְּתֵּיאָבוֹן—with hunger—since it represents the commitment of the Jew even though he is hungry. This constitutes the basic fulfillment of the mitzvah. Therefore, we recite עַל אֲכִילַת מַצָּה on the broken piece of matzah, which is the לֶחֶם עוֹנִי, and we eat it in a hungry state, as a deprived person would.

Rif and Rambam agree that the matzah represents commitment and faith, and that without these there can be no redemption, but they argue that the matzah also serves, especially in our times, as a kind of sacrificial offering at one's Seder. As we have pointed out, on Seder night the Jew is transposed to the Holy Temple of old. He wears the white *kittel*, he becomes a priest, he sits at his table of plenty with his family around him, singing songs, reclining, and drinking wine. But this also represents the greatest danger to Judaism because in the midst of plenty the Jew is most likely to forget those in need. He is even likely to forget God and to fall prey to assimilation. The real test of faith, the לַחְמָא דִמְהֵימְנוּתָא, comes then. Hence the fundamental mitzvah of matzah is to eat it עַל הַשּׂוֹבַע—in a state of satiety—and thus the *afikoman*.

TZAFUN

צָפוּן

THE AFIKOMAN

After the meal, the afikoman is distributed.

הִנְנִי מוּכָן וּמְזֻמָּן לְקַיֵּם מִצְוַת אֲכִילַת אֲפִיקוֹמָן, לְשֵׁם יִחוּד קוּדְשָׁא בְּרִיךְ־הוּא
וּשְׁכִינְתֵּיהּ עַל־יְדֵי הַהוּא טָמִיר וְנֶעְלָם בְּשֵׁם כָּל־יִשְׂרָאֵל:

The Origin of the Grace after Meals   בָּרֵךְ

The Grace after Meals consists of four blessings, the first three of which, according to the Talmud (*Berakhot* 48b), are based on biblical prescription. The biblical basis for these three blessings is not immediately obvious but can be readily discerned by a careful examination of Deuteronomy 8.

We begin with verse 3: "Not by bread alone does man live, but by that which comes forth from God's mouth does man live." Sustenance derives solely from man's efforts (symbolized by bread) but also and primarily from God's beneficence. Thus, in our first blessing in *birkat ha-mazon* we extol God as the Source of food—for all. He is a universal Provider of all His creatures: Jew and non-Jew, man as well as animal.

The biblical passage moves from the universal to the particular. In verse 10 we have "You shall eat and be satisfied and give thanks to the Lord thy God for the land He has given you." What is the connection between the land—an obvious reference to the land of Israel—and the food we eat? Do we not have to give thanks for our sustenance regardless of where we live? The answer of course is that we do, but true enjoyment of the food depends upon a sense of security. Only when we have our land and live thereon and are not dependent for food upon a foreign country can we offer full-hearted gratitude for our nourishment. Thus, the second blessing of *birkat ha-mazon* is devoted to the land that God has bestowed upon us.

Chapter 8 concludes with a warning that we not become haughty and conclude that our success is due to our own efforts. We may not forget that it is the Lord who brought us out of Egypt and who sustained us in the desert through the manna (vv. 14 and 16), and who supports us at all times and gives us strength to acquire our needs (v. 18). The land, which is but a physical entity, is not the ultimate source of our security. It is upon our spiritual strength—symbolized by Jerusalem—that we truly rely. "And all people of the earth shall see that you are called by the name of the Lord, and they shall fear you" (Deut. 28:10). The third, and last of the biblically-ordained blessings is, therefore, בּוֹנֶה יְרוּשָׁלַיִם—an offering of praise to God for building Jerusalem and making it the spiritual capital of the world and granting us, the Jew who live therein, spiritual strength and fortitude.

The fourth blessing, which concludes with הַטּוֹב וְהַמֵּטִיב, is rabbinic in origin. The Rabbis relate that this blessing was introduced after the unsuccessful Bar Kokhba rebellion against Rome, when the Hadrianic persecutions made it nearly possible for Jews to endure. Many Jews had been slain during the revolt, and—by a miracle of Divine beneficence—the Romans allowed the Jewish corpses to be buried. By a second miracle, the bodies had not decomposed even though the Jewish soldiers had been killed well before their burial was permitted. הַטּוֹב—God is good, for He allowed the bodies to be buried; הַמֵּטִיב—He does good because the bodies had not decomposed (*Berakhot* 48b). What an amazing testimony to Jewish faith in redemption. Job exclaimed, "Though he slay me, in Him shall I trust" (Job 13:15). At the very moment when all their aspirations to freedom had been dashed, the Jews created a fourth blessing for the Grace after Meals in gratitude to God for having preserved them, even in such a limited fashion. Only a people which still retained faith in ultimate redemption could fashion such a blessing. Most appropriately, the *birkat hamazon* at the Seder is followed by the Cup of Elijah.

BAREKH

בָּרֵךְ

GRACE AFTER THE MEAL

The third cup of wine is filled.

הָיִינוּ כְּחוֹלְמִים

When God returned us to Zion we were like dreamers. Only those who dreamed were ultimately redeemed. Show me what you dream, goes a well-known saying, and I will tell you not only what you are but what you can become. Joseph dreamed great cosmic dreams. Jacob, his father, knew that while those who dream may not see their dreams fulfilled, those who never dream have nothing to fulfill. Shakespeare wrote: "We are such stuff as dreams are made of." His line may be amended to: "We are such stuff as *our* dreams are made of."

The Gemara in chapter 9 of *Berakhot* lists several kinds of dreams that are "true dreams": a dream close to morning, a dream that is repeated again and again, and a dream whose interpretation is a part of the dream. The late Jewish scholar and sage Rabbi Samuel Kalman Mirsky (1899–1967) observed that what the Gemara is really teaching us is that if a dream is to be realized, it must be a dream of the dawn—a dream of redemption. It must be a positive, affirmative dream that inspires. It must be a dream that gives no rest, a dream that brings the same vision again and again. It must be a dream that has practical implementation and whose interpretation and realization are a part of it. Such a dream will come to pass in reality.

Such was the dream of the returnees during the time of Ezra and Nehemiah after King Cyrus of Persia gave permission to re-settle Judea and to build a Holy Temple. Full of vision and enthu-siasm, they dreamt of restoring the Land of Israel. Over and over they saw the same vision. It came to them replete with a program and a plan. Such was and is the dream of the modern builders of Zion. By settling the land and settling *in* the land, we are practically implementing our dreams. These dreams will surely be fulfilled.

שִׁיר הַמַּעֲלוֹת בְּשׁוּב יְיָ אֶת־שִׁיבַת צִיּוֹן הָיִינוּ כְּחֹלְמִים: אָז יִמָּלֵא שְׂחוֹק
פִּינוּ וּלְשׁוֹנֵנוּ רִנָּה. אָז יֹאמְרוּ בַגּוֹיִם הִגְדִּיל יְיָ לַעֲשׂוֹת עִם־אֵלֶּה: הִגְדִּיל
יְיָ לַעֲשׂוֹת עִמָּנוּ הָיִינוּ שְׂמֵחִים: שׁוּבָה יְיָ אֶת־שְׁבִיתֵנוּ כַּאֲפִיקִים בַּנֶּגֶב:
הַזֹּרְעִים בְּדִמְעָה בְּרִנָּה יִקְצֹרוּ: הָלוֹךְ יֵלֵךְ וּבָכֹה נֹשֵׂא מֶשֶׁךְ־הַזָּרַע. בֹּא־
יָבֹא בְרִנָּה נֹשֵׂא אֲלֻמֹּתָיו:

If three men or more are at the table, the Grace is preceded by the
following introductory phrases. When ten or more are present, the
words in parentheses are added.

הִנְנִי מוּכָן וּמְזֻמָּן לְקַיֵּם מִצְוַת עֲשֵׂה שֶׁל בִּרְכַּת הַמָּזוֹן. שֶׁנֶּאֱמַר: וְאָכַלְתָּ וְשָׂבָעְתָּ,
וּבֵרַכְתָּ אֶת־יְיָ אֱלֹהֶיךָ, עַל־הָאָרֶץ הַטֹּבָה אֲשֶׁר נָתַן־לָךְ: לְשֵׁם יִחוּד קוּדְשָׁא
בְּרִיךְ־הוּא וּשְׁכִינְתֵּיהּ עַל־יְדֵי הַהוּא טָמִיר וְנֶעְלָם בְּשֵׁם כָּל־יִשְׂרָאֵל:

הַמְזַמֵּן אוֹמֵר: רַבּוֹתַי נְבָרֵךְ:

הַמְסֻבִּים עוֹנִים: יְהִי שֵׁם יְיָ מְבֹרָךְ מֵעַתָּה וְעַד עוֹלָם:

הַמְזַמֵּן: יְהִי שֵׁם יְיָ מְבֹרָךְ מֵעַתָּה וְעַד עוֹלָם:

הַמְזַמֵּן: בִּרְשׁוּת מָרָנָן וְרַבָּנָן וְרַבּוֹתַי, נְבָרֵךְ (אֱלֹהֵינוּ) שֶׁאָכַלְנוּ מִשֶּׁלּוֹ:

הַמְסֻבִּים עוֹנִים: בָּרוּךְ (אֱלֹהֵינוּ) שֶׁאָכַלְנוּ מִשֶּׁלּוֹ וּבְטוּבוֹ חָיִינוּ:

הַמְזַמֵּן: בָּרוּךְ (אֱלֹהֵינוּ) שֶׁאָכַלְנוּ מִשֶּׁלּוֹ וּבְטוּבוֹ חָיִינוּ:

הַמְזַמֵּן: בָּרוּךְ הוּא וּבָרוּךְ שְׁמוֹ:

If less than three men are present, begin here:

בָּרוּךְ אַתָּה יְיָ, אֱלֹהֵינוּ מֶלֶךְ הָעוֹלָם, הַזָּן אֶת־הָעוֹלָם כֻּלּוֹ, בְּטוּבוֹ, בְּחֵן
בְּחֶסֶד וּבְרַחֲמִים, הוּא נוֹתֵן לֶחֶם לְכָל־בָּשָׂר כִּי לְעוֹלָם חַסְדּוֹ. וּבְטוּבוֹ
הַגָּדוֹל, תָּמִיד לֹא־חָסַר לָנוּ, וְאַל־יֶחְסַר לָנוּ מָזוֹן לְעוֹלָם וָעֶד. בַּעֲבוּר
שְׁמוֹ הַגָּדוֹל, כִּי הוּא אֵל זָן וּמְפַרְנֵס לַכֹּל וּמֵטִיב לַכֹּל וּמֵכִין מָזוֹן לְכָל־
בְּרִיּוֹתָיו אֲשֶׁר בָּרָא: בָּרוּךְ אַתָּה יְיָ, הַזָּן אֶת־הַכֹּל:

A Pilgrim Song. When the Eternal brought the exiles back to Zion we were as in a dream. Our mouth was filled with laughter and our tongue with song. The nations said: The Eternal has done great things for them. Yes, the Eternal did great things for us and we were very happy. Restore our good fortune, O Eternal, as dry streams that flow again. They that sow in tears shall reap in joy. Though the planter may weep as he carries seed to the field, he will yet return with joy, bearing the sheaves of grain.

If three men or more are at the table, the Grace is preceded by the following introductory phrases. When ten or more are present, the words in parentheses are added.

The leader: Let us say grace.
Those assembled: May the name of the Eternal be blessed from now and for evermore.
The leader repeats the preceding sentence and continues:
With the permission of all present, let us praise Him (our God) Whose food we have eaten.
Those assembled: Blessed be He (our God) Whose food we have eaten and in Whose goodness we live.
The leader repeats the preceding sentence and continues:
Blessed be He and blessed be His name.

If less than three men are present, begin here:

Blessed art Thou, Eternal our God, Ruler of the universe, Who sustains the whole universe in His goodness, with grace, loving-kindness and mercy. He gives food to all, for His mercy endures forever. In His great goodness He never failed us with sustenance, and may He never fail us, forever and ever, for the sake of His great name. It is He Who provides for all, sustains all and is beneficent to all, preparing food for all His creatures whom He created. Blessed art Thou, Eternal, Who provides food for all.

נוֹדֶה לְּךָ יְיָ אֱלֹהֵינוּ עַל שֶׁהִנְחַלְתָּ לַאֲבוֹתֵינוּ, אֶרֶץ חֶמְדָּה טוֹבָה וּרְחָבָה. וְעַל שֶׁהוֹצֵאתָנוּ, יְיָ אֱלֹהֵינוּ, מֵאֶרֶץ מִצְרַיִם, וּפְדִיתָנוּ מִבֵּית עֲבָדִים. וְעַל בְּרִיתְךָ שֶׁחָתַמְתָּ בִּבְשָׂרֵנוּ, וְעַל תּוֹרָתְךָ שֶׁלִּמַּדְתָּנוּ, וְעַל חֻקֶּיךָ שֶׁהוֹדַעְתָּנוּ, וְעַל חַיִּים חֵן וָחֶסֶד שֶׁחוֹנַנְתָּנוּ, וְעַל אֲכִילַת מָזוֹן שֶׁאַתָּה זָן וּמְפַרְנֵס אוֹתָנוּ תָּמִיד, בְּכָל־יוֹם וּבְכָל־עֵת וּבְכָל־שָׁעָה:

וְעַל הַכֹּל יְיָ אֱלֹהֵינוּ, אֲנַחְנוּ מוֹדִים לָךְ, וּמְבָרְכִים אוֹתָךְ, יִתְבָּרַךְ שִׁמְךָ, בְּפִי כָל־חַי, תָּמִיד לְעוֹלָם וָעֶד. כַּכָּתוּב, וְאָכַלְתָּ וְשָׂבָעְתָּ, וּבֵרַכְתָּ אֶת־יְיָ אֱלֹהֶיךָ, עַל־הָאָרֶץ הַטֹּבָה אֲשֶׁר־נָתַן לָךְ: בָּרוּךְ אַתָּה יְיָ, עַל הָאָרֶץ וְעַל הַמָּזוֹן:

רַחֶם־נָא יְיָ אֱלֹהֵינוּ, עַל יִשְׂרָאֵל עַמֶּךָ, וְעַל יְרוּשָׁלַיִם עִירֶךָ, וְעַל צִיּוֹן מִשְׁכַּן כְּבוֹדֶךָ, וְעַל מַלְכוּת בֵּית דָּוִד מְשִׁיחֶךָ, וְעַל הַבַּיִת הַגָּדוֹל וְהַקָּדוֹשׁ שֶׁנִּקְרָא שִׁמְךָ עָלָיו. אֱלֹהֵינוּ, אָבִינוּ, רְעֵנוּ, זוּנֵנוּ, פַּרְנְסֵנוּ, וְכַלְכְּלֵנוּ, וְהַרְוִיחֵנוּ. וְהַרְוַח־לָנוּ יְיָ אֱלֹהֵינוּ מְהֵרָה מִכָּל־צָרוֹתֵינוּ. וְנָא, אַל־תַּצְרִיכֵנוּ יְיָ אֱלֹהֵינוּ לֹא לִידֵי מַתְּנַת בָּשָׂר וָדָם, וְלֹא לִידֵי הַלְוָאָתָם, כִּי אִם לְיָדְךָ הַמְּלֵאָה, הַפְּתוּחָה, הַקְּדוֹשָׁה וְהָרְחָבָה, שֶׁלֹּא נֵבוֹשׁ וְלֹא נִכָּלֵם לְעוֹלָם וָעֶד:

The following paragraph is added on the Sabbath:

רְצֵה וְהַחֲלִיצֵנוּ יְיָ אֱלֹהֵינוּ, בְּמִצְוֹתֶיךָ, וּבְמִצְוַת יוֹם הַשְּׁבִיעִי הַשַּׁבָּת הַגָּדוֹל וְהַקָּדוֹשׁ הַזֶּה. כִּי יוֹם זֶה, גָּדוֹל וְקָדוֹשׁ הוּא לְפָנֶיךָ, לִשְׁבָּת בּוֹ וְלָנוּחַ בּוֹ, בְּאַהֲבָה, כְּמִצְוַת רְצוֹנֶךָ. וּבִרְצוֹנְךָ הָנִיחַ לָנוּ יְיָ אֱלֹהֵינוּ, שֶׁלֹּא תְהֵא צָרָה וְיָגוֹן וַאֲנָחָה, בְּיוֹם מְנוּחָתֵנוּ. וְהַרְאֵנוּ, יְיָ אֱלֹהֵינוּ, בְּנֶחָמַת צִיּוֹן עִירֶךָ, וּבְבִנְיַן יְרוּשָׁלַיִם עִיר קָדְשֶׁךָ, כִּי אַתָּה הוּא, בַּעַל הַיְשׁוּעוֹת, וּבַעַל הַנֶּחָמוֹת:

We thank You, Eternal our God, for the goodly land which You gave to our forefathers; and for bringing us out from the land of Egypt, O Eternal our God, and redeeming us from the house of bondage; and for Your covenant sealed in our flesh; and for Your Torah which You taught us; and for Your laws which You made known to us; and for the life of grace and loving-kindness which You have graciously bestowed upon us; and for the food we eat with which You nourish and sustain us at all times, daily, and at every season and at every hour.

For all these blessings, Eternal our God, we thank You and bless You. May Your name be blessed in the mouths of all the living at all times and for all time! Thus do we fulfill Your command: "Thou shalt eat and be satisfied, and bless the Eternal your God for the goodly land which He has given thee." Blessed art Thou, Eternal, for the land and for our sustenance.

Eternal our God, have mercy on Israel Your people, on Jerusalem Your city and Zion the dwelling place of Your glory, on the royal house of David Your anointed, and on the great and holy Temple called by Your name. Our God, our Father, be Thou our Shepherd. Sustain us, support us and provide for all our needs, and Eternal our God, give us speedy relief from all our troubles. Eternal our God, may we never be brought to depend on gifts or loans from the hand of flesh and blood, but only on Your hand, full, open, abundant and generous. Thus shall we never be put to shame.

The following paragraph is added on the Sabbath:

Eternal our God, by Your grace, strengthen us in Your commandments, particularly in the observance of the seventh day, this great and holy Sabbath. For it is a great and holy day given by You in love for rest and serenity. May it be Your will, Eternal our God, to grant us such repose that there shall be no sorrow, trouble or sighing on our day of rest. And, Eternal our God, may we see Zion Your city comforted, Jerusalem Your holy city rebuilt, for You are the God of salvation and consolation.

אֱלֹהֵינוּ וֵאלֹהֵי אֲבוֹתֵינוּ, יַעֲלֶה וְיָבֹא, וְיַגִּיעַ, וְיֵרָאֶה, וְיֵרָצֶה, וְיִשָּׁמַע, וְיִפָּקֵד, וְיִזָּכֵר, זִכְרוֹנֵנוּ וּפִקְדוֹנֵנוּ, וְזִכְרוֹן אֲבוֹתֵינוּ, וְזִכְרוֹן מָשִׁיחַ בֶּן־דָּוִד עַבְדֶּךָ, וְזִכְרוֹן יְרוּשָׁלַיִם עִיר קָדְשֶׁךָ, וְזִכְרוֹן כָּל־עַמְּךָ בֵּית יִשְׂרָאֵל, לְפָנֶיךָ. לִפְלֵיטָה, לְטוֹבָה, לְחֵן וּלְחֶסֶד וּלְרַחֲמִים, לְחַיִּים וּלְשָׁלוֹם, בְּיוֹם חַג הַמַּצּוֹת הַזֶּה. זָכְרֵנוּ יְיָ אֱלֹהֵינוּ, בּוֹ לְטוֹבָה, וּפָקְדֵנוּ בוֹ לִבְרָכָה, וְהוֹשִׁיעֵנוּ בוֹ לְחַיִּים טוֹבִים. וּבִדְבַר יְשׁוּעָה וְרַחֲמִים, חוּס וְחָנֵּנוּ, וְרַחֵם עָלֵינוּ וְהוֹשִׁיעֵנוּ, כִּי אֵלֶיךָ עֵינֵינוּ, כִּי אֵל מֶלֶךְ חַנּוּן וְרַחוּם אָתָּה:

וּבְנֵה יְרוּשָׁלַיִם עִיר הַקֹּדֶשׁ, בִּמְהֵרָה בְּיָמֵינוּ: בָּרוּךְ אַתָּה יְיָ, בּוֹנֶה בְרַחֲמָיו יְרוּשָׁלַיִם. אָמֵן:

בָּרוּךְ אַתָּה יְיָ, אֱלֹהֵינוּ מֶלֶךְ הָעוֹלָם, הָאֵל אָבִינוּ, מַלְכֵּנוּ, אַדִּירֵנוּ, בּוֹרְאֵנוּ, גּוֹאֲלֵנוּ, יוֹצְרֵנוּ, קְדוֹשֵׁנוּ, קְדוֹשׁ יַעֲקֹב. רוֹעֵנוּ רֹעֵה יִשְׂרָאֵל. הַמֶּלֶךְ הַטּוֹב, וְהַמֵּטִיב לַכֹּל, שֶׁבְּכָל־יוֹם וָיוֹם הוּא הֵטִיב, הוּא מֵטִיב, הוּא יֵיטִיב לָנוּ: הוּא גְמָלָנוּ. הוּא גוֹמְלֵנוּ. הוּא יִגְמְלֵנוּ לָעַד. לְחֵן וּלְחֶסֶד, וּלְרַחֲמִים וּלְרֶוַח. הַצָּלָה וְהַצְלָחָה. בְּרָכָה וִישׁוּעָה. נֶחָמָה, פַּרְנָסָה וְכַלְכָּלָה. וְרַחֲמִים, וְחַיִּים וְשָׁלוֹם, וְכָל־טוֹב, וּמִכָּל־טוּב לְעוֹלָם אַל יְחַסְּרֵנוּ: הָרַחֲמָן, הוּא יִמְלֹךְ עָלֵינוּ לְעוֹלָם וָעֶד: הָרַחֲמָן, הוּא יִתְבָּרַךְ בַּשָּׁמַיִם וּבָאָרֶץ: הָרַחֲמָן, הוּא יִשְׁתַּבַּח לְדוֹר דּוֹרִים, וְיִתְפָּאַר בָּנוּ לָעַד וּלְנֵצַח נְצָחִים, וְיִתְהַדַּר בָּנוּ לָעַד וּלְעוֹלְמֵי עוֹלָמִים: הָרַחֲמָן, הוּא יְפַרְנְסֵנוּ בְּכָבוֹד: הָרַחֲמָן, הוּא יִשְׁבֹּר עֻלֵּנוּ מֵעַל צַוָּארֵנוּ, וְהוּא יוֹלִיכֵנוּ קוֹמְמִיּוּת לְאַרְצֵנוּ: הָרַחֲמָן, הוּא יִשְׁלַח לָנוּ, בְּרָכָה מְרֻבָּה בַּבַּיִת הַזֶּה, וְעַל שֻׁלְחָן זֶה שֶׁאָכַלְנוּ עָלָיו: הָרַחֲמָן, הוּא יִשְׁלַח לָנוּ, אֶת־אֵלִיָּהוּ הַנָּבִיא זָכוּר לַטּוֹב וִיבַשֶּׂר־לָנוּ בְּשׂוֹרוֹת טוֹבוֹת יְשׁוּעוֹת וְנֶחָמוֹת:

Our God and God of our fathers, on this day of the Festival of Matzot may there come before You the remembrance of us and our fathers, of Jerusalem Your holy city, of the Messiah the son of David Your servant, and of all Your people of the house of Israel. May these come before You, and in tenderness, grace and mercy be heard and accepted with favor by You for life and peace, for deliverance and happiness. Eternal our God, remember us this day for happiness, for blessing and the good life. With a word of salvation and mercy have pity on us and save us. Our eyes are lifted toward Thee, for Thou art a gracious and merciful God and King.

O rebuild Jerusalem the holy city soon in our days! Blessed art Thou, Eternal, Who will rebuild Jerusalem in His mercy. Amen.

Blessed art Thou, Eternal our God, Ruler of the universe, God our Father, our King, our Mighty One, our Creator, our Redeem-er, our Maker, our Holy One, the Holy One of Jacob, our Shepherd and Shepherd of Israel, the good King Who does good to all. Even as He has daily done good to us, so may He continue to do good to us forever. Even as He has dealt bountifully with us, so may He ever bestow upon us with boundless grace, loving-kindness and mercy, help, prosperity, blessing, salvation, conso-lation, sustenance and support, in life and peace and all that is good. And may we never know lack of anything good.

May the All-merciful rule over us forever.

May the All-merciful be blessed in the heavens and on the earth.

May the All-merciful be praised for all generations and glori-fied and honored among us for all eternity.

May the All-merciful grant that our needs be supplied with dignity.

May the All-merciful break the oppressor's yoke from our neck and lead us proudly to our land.

May the All-merciful send the fullness of blessing on this household and bless this table at which we have eaten.

May the All-merciful send to us the prophet Elijah, of blessed memory, bearing good tidings of deliverance and comfort.

הָרַחֲמָן, הוּא יְבָרֵךְ (אם יש לו אב ואם יאמר) אֶת־אָבִי מוֹרִי בַּעַל הַבַּיִת הַזֶּה,
וְאֶת־אִמִּי מוֹרָתִי, בַּעֲלַת הַבַּיִת הַזֶּה. (ואם הוא נשוי יאמר) אוֹתִי וְאֶת אִשְׁתִּי
וְאֶת זַרְעִי וְאֶת־כָּל־אֲשֶׁר לִי. אוֹתָם וְאֶת־בֵּיתָם, וְאֶת־זַרְעָם וְאֶת־כָּל־
אֲשֶׁר לָהֶם. אוֹתָנוּ וְאֶת־כָּל־אֲשֶׁר לָנוּ, כְּמוֹ שֶׁנִּתְבָּרְכוּ אֲבוֹתֵינוּ,
אַבְרָהָם, יִצְחָק וְיַעֲקֹב, בַּכֹּל, מִכֹּל, כֹּל. כֵּן יְבָרֵךְ אוֹתָנוּ, כֻּלָּנוּ יַחַד,
בִּבְרָכָה שְׁלֵמָה. וְנֹאמַר אָמֵן:

בַּמָּרוֹם יְלַמְּדוּ עֲלֵיהֶם וְעָלֵינוּ זְכוּת, שֶׁתְּהֵא לְמִשְׁמֶרֶת שָׁלוֹם, וְנִשָּׂא
בְרָכָה מֵאֵת יְיָ, וּצְדָקָה מֵאֱלֹהֵי יִשְׁעֵנוּ. וְנִמְצָא חֵן וְשֵׂכֶל טוֹב בְּעֵינֵי
אֱלֹהִים וְאָדָם:

The following sentence is added on the Sabbath:

הָרַחֲמָן, הוּא יַנְחִילֵנוּ יוֹם שֶׁכֻּלּוֹ שַׁבָּת וּמְנוּחָה, לְחַיֵּי הָעוֹלָמִים:

הָרַחֲמָן, הוּא יַנְחִילֵנוּ יוֹם שֶׁכֻּלּוֹ טוֹב:

הָרַחֲמָן, הוּא יְזַכֵּנוּ לִימוֹת הַמָּשִׁיחַ וּלְחַיֵּי הָעוֹלָם הַבָּא. מִגְדּוֹל יְשׁוּעוֹת
מַלְכּוֹ, וְעֹשֶׂה חֶסֶד לִמְשִׁיחוֹ, לְדָוִד וּלְזַרְעוֹ עַד עוֹלָם. עֹשֶׂה שָׁלוֹם
בִּמְרוֹמָיו, הוּא יַעֲשֶׂה שָׁלוֹם, עָלֵינוּ וְעַל כָּל יִשְׂרָאֵל, וְאִמְרוּ אָמֵן:

יְראוּ אֶת־יְיָ קְדֹשָׁיו, כִּי אֵין מַחְסוֹר לִירֵאָיו: כְּפִירִים רָשׁוּ וְרָעֵבוּ,
וְדֹרְשֵׁי־יְיָ לֹא־יַחְסְרוּ כָל־טוֹב: הוֹדוּ לַיְיָ כִּי טוֹב, כִּי לְעוֹלָם חַסְדּוֹ:
פּוֹתֵחַ אֶת־יָדֶךָ, וּמַשְׂבִּיעַ לְכָל־חַי רָצוֹן: בָּרוּךְ הַגֶּבֶר אֲשֶׁר יִבְטַח בַּיְיָ,
וְהָיָה יְיָ מִבְטַחוֹ: נַעַר הָיִיתִי, גַּם זָקַנְתִּי, וְלֹא רָאִיתִי צַדִּיק נֶעֱזָב, וְזַרְעוֹ
מְבַקֶּשׁ־לָחֶם: יְיָ עֹז לְעַמּוֹ יִתֵּן, יְיָ יְבָרֵךְ אֶת־עַמּוֹ בַשָּׁלוֹם:

May the All-merciful bless this house and all assembled here, us and all that is ours. May He bless us all together with perfect blessing, even as our ancestors Abraham, Isaac and Jacob were blessed with every manner of blessing, and let us say, Amen.

On high may there be invoked for them and for us such grace as shall ever be a safeguard of peace. Then shall we receive blessing from the Eternal and righteousness from the God of our salvation, and may we find grace and understanding in the eyes of God and of man.

The following sentence is added on the Sabbath:

May the All-merciful grant us a day that shall be altogether Sabbath and repose in eternal life.

May the All-merciful grant us a day that shall be altogether good.

May the All-merciful make us worthy of seeing the days of the Messiah and life in the world to come. He is a tower of salvation to His king and shows kindness to His anointed, to David and his seed forever. May the Creator of harmony in the heavens create peace for us and for all Israel, and let us say, Amen.

Venerate the Eternal, you His holy ones, for those who revere Him suffer no want. Even young lions may lack and know hunger, but they who seek the Eternal shall not lack any good. Give thanks unto the Eternal for He is good. For His mercy endures for ever. Thou openest Thy hand and satisfiest every living thing. Blessed is the man who trusts in the Eternal, and the Eternal is his stronghold. I have been young, now I am old; and I have not seen a righteous man forsaken or his children begging for bread. The Eternal will give strength to His people; the Eternal will bless His people with peace.

THE THIRD CUP

כּוֹס שְׁלִישִׁית

הִנְנִי מוּכָן וּמְזֻמָּן לְקַיֵּים מִצְוַת כּוֹס שְׁלִישִׁית מֵאַרְבַּע כּוֹסוֹת לְשֵׁם יִחוּד קוּדְשָׁא בְּרִיךְ־הוּא וּשְׁכִינְתֵּיה עַל־יְדֵי הַהוּא טָמִיר וְנֶעְלָם בְּשֵׁם כָּל־יִשְׂרָאֵל.

Blessed art Thou, Eternal our God, Ruler of the universe, Creator of the fruit of the vine.

בָּרוּךְ אַתָּה יְיָ, אֱלֹהֵינוּ מֶלֶךְ הָעוֹלָם, בּוֹרֵא פְּרִי הַגָּפֶן:

Drink the third cup of wine while leaning to the left.

The Cup of Elijah

כּוֹס אֵלִיָּהוּ

Before the fourth cup of wine is poured, a special cup of wine filled to overflowing is set at the center of the table for the prophet Elijah. The front door is opened and everyone rises to recite one of the most incongruous passages in the Haggadah: שְׁפֹךְ חֲמָתְךָ אֶל הַגּוֹיִם אֲשֶׁר לֹא יְדָעוּךָ.

Several questions can be raised immediately. Why do we open the door at this moment and not at the beginning of the Seder, when we invited all the strangers to come in? Why must we open the door for Elijah, for if he can manage to visit each person's Seder in one night, he can surely come through a closed door? And further, what a strange greeting! As we welcome the forerunner of the Messiah, we pronounce what appears to be a malediction upon the nations of the world.

In response to these questions, we must realize that the Haggadah reflects all of Jewish history. Because of its proximity to Easter, the Passover season was always a very difficult period for the Jews. It was a time of popular excitement about the death of Jesus, which was blamed upon the Jews and was constantly exploited by the Christian clergy to fan anti-Jewish hatred. Passover was the season for reviving the blood libel that accused Jews of killing gentile babies and using their blood to prepare the matzah and the wine for the Seder. On Seder night the gentiles often staged vicious pogroms against their Jewish neighbors, making it necessary to open the door and look out into the street, lest, God forbid, a dead baby had been placed near the house to provide the mob with a pretext to ravage and kill. It was not at all rare to see Jewish families driven from their homes and Jewish populations from their villages in the middle of Seder night to escape certain injury and even death. Heinrich Heine tells such a story in his *The Rabbi of Bacharach.*

The reciting of שְׁפֹךְ חֲמָתְךָ need not be explained only on the basis of medieval Jewish history with its vicious anti-Jewish violence. The notion of God as the Redeemer of Jewish blood goes back to the Exodus itself. It was then that Amalek, Israel's archenemy and the prototype of the Jew-killer from Haman to Hitler, attacked the Jews during their march through the desert. Instead of fighting the able-bodied, he attacked the rear guard—the aged, the women, and the children. With the help of God, Israel defeated Amalek in a memorable battle, after which the Almighty said to Moses, "I will utterly blot out the memory of Amalek from under Heaven" (Ex. 17:14). While we are in the desert of the exile, totally exposed to the depredations of our enemies, we must rely upon God to take the role of *go'el* (redeemer) and to save us from our enemies. Thus, while the Exodus primarily recalls the redemption from Egypt, it also reminds us of the enemies on the outside who did not fail to attack us and thereby try to snuff out the redemption. We, therefore, beseech God to save us from them and pour his wrath upon them for their attempts to destroy His holy people—as Amalek tried when we left Egypt.

The spirit of active revenge is alien to Israel. Israel's essential, God-given quest is for universal peace and justice. In the past the "religion of love" constantly pursued its antagonists, and those it considered "not of the faith," with fire and sword, with the horrors of the Inquisition and the burning stake. Unlike Judaism, it claims that there is no salvation outside its own congregation. Jews, on the other hand, believe that all people, regardless of their religion, merit salvation as long as they believe in one God and act morally. The plea that "God pour out His wrath" is not directed to non-Jewish religions but to those people who destroy Jewish lives.

Why must we open the door for Elijah the Prophet? Because, unless *we* open the door, Elijah will not come. There is a fundamental difference between the initial redemption and the ultimate redemption. The initial redemption from Egypt was wrought by God alone. He brought about the Ten Plagues; He parted the Red Sea; and He fought Pharaoh's armies. We were still slaves and could not act on our own. But when God gave us the Torah and we stood at Sinai and cried out נַעֲשֶׂה וְנִשְׁמַע—"we will act and we will attempt to understand"—we took the responsibility for ultimate redemption upon ourselves. It is we who now must act to bring Elijah, the precursor of Messiah. As the Kotzker Rebbe said, "Where is the place of God's glory? Wherever one allows Him in." At the very least we must rise from our table and let Elijah in. If we only open the door, redemption will come in our time.

Fill the cup of Elijah the Prophet and open the door. All rise.

Pour out Thy wrath upon the nations that know Thee not, and upon the kingdoms that call not upon Thy name; for they have consumed Jacob and laid waste his habitation. Pour out Thy rage upon them and let Thy fury overtake them. Pursue them in anger and destroy them from under the heavens of the Eternal.

שְׁפֹךְ חֲמָתְךָ אֶל־הַגּוֹיִם אֲשֶׁר לֹא־יְדָעוּךָ, וְעַל־מַמְלָכוֹת אֲשֶׁר בְּשִׁמְךָ לֹא קָרָאוּ: כִּי אָכַל אֶת־יַעֲקֹב וְאֶת־נָוֵהוּ הֵשַׁמּוּ: שְׁפָךְ־עֲלֵיהֶם זַעְמֶךָ וַחֲרוֹן אַפְּךָ יַשִּׂיגֵם: תִּרְדֹּף בְּאַף וְתַשְׁמִידֵם, מִתַּחַת שְׁמֵי יְיָ:

Close the door. All are seated.

At many Seders, at this point, before *Hallel*, the Six Million who perished in the Holocaust are remembered with a song dedicated to their memory, *Ani Ma'amin*. This is often followed by the song *Kahol ve-Lavan* (כָּחוֹל וְלָבָן), first sung by Ruth Alexandrovitch, a young Russian girl who dreamed of the blue-and-white freedom flag of Israel, in honor of the three million Jews behind the Iron Curtain who cannot celebrate a Seder in freedom and openness.

HALLEL   הַלֵּל

We now commence the second half of *Hallel*. We noted above that *Hallel* on the Seder night is unusual in that it is interrupted by the meal. On all other occasions when we recite this thanksgiving prayer, we are most careful not to allow any interruptions, but at the Seder we purposely divide the *Hallel* into two and we eat in between. This anomaly indicates, as has often been said, that the Seder repast is not an ordinary meal; it is, in essence, a kind of *hallel* unto itself. Surely this was so during the time of the Temple, when the paschal sacrifice was the central feature of the meal. Our consumption thereof was, in and of itself, a form of thanksgiving to the Almighty. But even in our time, the meal, accompanied by the eating of matzah and *maror*, effused with songs of joy, and elevated with Torah discussion, is a form of *Hallel* and is thus a link between the two parts of this prayer.

The ending of the *Hallel* is also noteworthy. On other occasions the six psalms that constitute *Hallel* are followed by the brief ending of יְהַלְלוּךְ. On the Seder night, however, instead of ending with this customary paragraph, we continue with the psalm beginning הוֹדוּ לה' כִּי טוֹב (Ps. 136:1), which is called הַלֵּל הַגָּדוֹל—the Great *Hallel*. This in turn is followed by נִשְׁמַת, שׁוֹכֵן עַד and יִשְׁתַּבַּח, which are festival morning prayers. Only then do we end with יְהַלְלוּךְ. What purpose do these additional psalms and prayers serve? An examination of a talmudic passage in *Pesaḥim* might shed some light on this problem.

The Mishnah states: "Wine is poured for the third cup and *birkat ha-mazon* (Grace after Meals) is recited over it. [Afterwards] the fourth cup is poured and upon it we conclude the *Hallel* and recite the בִּרְכַּת הַשִׁיר [literally, "the blessing of the song"]" (*Pes.* 10:5). In the Gemara there is a discussion of the meaning of the term בִּרְכַּת הַשִׁיר. R. Yehuda opines that it refers to יְהַלְלוּךְ ה' אֱלֹקֵינוּ, the usual ending of *Hallel*. R. Yoḥanan counters that it is נִשְׁמַת כָּל חַי, the prayer that completes the Sabbath and holiday *pesukei de-zimra*. The latter opinion, which we generally follow, is rather perplexing since it implies that *Hallel* by itself is insufficient and must be followed by נִשְׁמַת כָּל חַי. What theme does the latter contain which is not already in the former? Moreover, if the two series of prayers are indeed different, should not each one be recited over its own cup of wine?

The answer to these questions lies in the very next statement in the Gemara (*Pes.* 118a), which reads as follows: תָּנוּ רַבָּנָן רְבִיעִי גוֹמֵר עָלָיו אֶת הַהַלֵּל וְאוֹמֵר הַלֵּל הַגָּדוֹל, דִּבְרֵי ר"ט, "It was taught by the Rabbis that on the fourth cup one completes the *Hallel* and then recites the Great *Hallel*. Such is the opinion of R. Tarphon." Tosafot (*Pes.* 117b, s.v. רְבִיעִי), as well as other Rishonim, refer to a variant reading of the text. Instead of כּוֹס רְבִיעִי (the fourth cup), the text reads כּוֹס חַמִישִׁי (the fifth cup). While voicing objection to this variant, these Rishonim nevertheless acknowledge its existence. Other early authorities, such as R. Ḥananel, actually seem to prefer the reading of כּוֹס חַמִישִׁי.

The suggestion that there are five cups at the Seder table immediately strikes a chord, for there are indeed five expressions of redemption—not four—that correspond to the cups of wine we drink. Earlier we mentioned the four as וְהוֹצֵאתִי, וְהִצַּלְתִּי, וְגָאַלְתִּי and וְלָקַחְתִּי—"I will take you out," "I will save you," "I will redeem you," and "I will take you" (Ex. 6:6–7). The fifth one, in the very next verse, is וְהֵבֵאתִי, "I will bring you to the land that I have promised Abraham, Isaac, and Jacob and I will give it to you as an inheritance."

The reference to a fifth cup did not go unnoticed by the *Posekim*. R. Asher (Rosh), an important halakhist of the fourteenth century, suggests—in recognition of the variant reading—that a fifth cup of wine be drunk, but that it be voluntary. The same opinion is held by Maimonides ("Laws of Leavened and Unleavened Bread" 8:10). The *Shulḥan Arukh* concurs with the aforementioned opinion, but is more restrictive in whom it allows to drink a fifth cup.° If one does pour and drink a fifth cup of wine, the halakhic authorities maintain that it is to be done over *hallel ha-gadol*, as is indicated in the Talmud.

The recitation of *hallel ha-gadol* over a fifth cup fits in very well with the order of the Seder. It provides a certain direction to the entire ceremony. We have already pointed out that the first half of the Seder, consisting mainly of *maggid*, is concerned with the redemption from Egypt—with the past. To be sure, the Seder is designed to make us feel that we ourselves are being redeemed—

° Only someone with a need or craving for more wine may have an additional cup (*Oraḥ Ḥayyim* 481:1) today—but the plain sense of the words and prayers speaks of the past. Indeed we close *maggid* with the first two psalms of *Hallel*, which refer specifically to the Exodus from Egypt. The final blessing of *maggid*, over the second cup of wine, provides a transition to the second half of *Hallel*, which we recite after the meal. In the blessing we extol God as our past and—even more so—future Redeemer, but we conclude it with גָּאַל יִשְׂרָאֵל, "Blessed is God who redeemed Israel"—in the past tense. The meal itself also serves as a transition between the past and the future. It is a reminder of the paschal lamb brought long ago when the Temple stood, but it also reflects our hope that in the future the Temple will be rebuilt.

After the repast, our focus shifts to the future: to our redemption to be. We pour a cup for Elijah, the harbinger of the Messiah and the symbol of Jewish renascence on our own land. The psalms of *Hallel* which follow speak of salvation and prosperity and of Jerusalem and our restoration to the Holy Land.

With the end of *Hallel*, we could have drunk the fourth cup and concluded the Seder, but the Rabbis insisted that we recite *hallel ha-gadol* and, according to some, even drink a fifth cup thereon. The basic theme of this *Hallel* and the accompanying prayers normally recited on the Sabbath and holidays is universal recognition of God's sovereignty. While the standard *Hallel* is concerned primarily with national redemption, the Great *Hallel* deals with universal redemption. The former is not enough, for our God is not only the God of Israel but also the God of the entire world, as the Almighty said to Abraham, "Through you shall all the families of the earth be blessed" (Gen. 12:3). In the *Aleinu* prayer, which we recite thrice daily, we assert that our task is לְתַקֵּן עוֹלָם בְּמַלְכוּת שַׁדַּי, "to perfect the *world* through the kingship of the Almighty." Our messianic hope is the moment of כִּי מִצִּיּוֹן תֵּצֵא תוֹרָה, "from Zion shall go forth the word of God" (Is. 2:3). It shall go forth to the entire world. Our task is to teach society the messianic dream of world freedom. This is the idea that underlies the refrain we repeat again and again: הוֹדוּ לַה' כִּי לְעוֹלָם חַסְדּוֹ, "His loving-kindness is forever" or, alternatively, "His loving-kindness is for the world."° It is not limited to Israel. "[God] gives bread to all flesh" (Ps. 136:25). Therefore, "Give thanks unto God of heaven " (Ps. 136:26). We conclude with נִשְׁמַת כָּל חַי in which we pray not only

° עוֹלָם has a dual meaning in Hebrew. It can mean "forever" or "the world."

that the Jews praise the God of Israel, but that all nations do so, as He is King over heaven and earth, יְשַׁתַּח שְׁמְךָ לָעַד מַלְכֵּנוּ.

Hence, the first part of the Seder deals with the Exodus from Egypt, and the second part treats the ideals of national and universal redemption. The Jewish people understand that only when the world is redeemed will *they* be redeemed. The redemption of Israel is bound up in the goodwill of the world, and the goodwill

הַלֵּל

The fourth cup is filled.

לֹא לָנוּ יְיָ, לֹא לָנוּ, כִּי־לְשִׁמְךָ תֵּן כָּבוֹד. עַל־חַסְדְּךָ עַל־אֲמִתֶּךָ: לָמָּה יֹאמְרוּ הַגּוֹיִם, אַיֵּה־נָא אֱלֹהֵיהֶם: וֵאלֹהֵינוּ בַשָּׁמָיִם, כֹּל אֲשֶׁר־חָפֵץ עָשָׂה: עֲצַבֵּיהֶם כֶּסֶף וְזָהָב, מַעֲשֵׂה יְדֵי אָדָם: פֶּה לָהֶם וְלֹא יְדַבֵּרוּ, עֵינַיִם לָהֶם וְלֹא יִרְאוּ: אָזְנַיִם לָהֶם וְלֹא יִשְׁמָעוּ, אַף לָהֶם וְלֹא יְרִיחוּן: יְדֵיהֶם וְלֹא יְמִישׁוּן, רַגְלֵיהֶם וְלֹא יְהַלֵּכוּ, לֹא־יֶהְגּוּ בִּגְרוֹנָם: כְּמוֹהֶם יִהְיוּ עֹשֵׂיהֶם, כֹּל אֲשֶׁר־בֹּטֵחַ בָּהֶם: יִשְׂרָאֵל בְּטַח בַּיְיָ, עֶזְרָם וּמָגִנָּם הוּא: בֵּית אַהֲרֹן בִּטְחוּ בַיְיָ. עֶזְרָם וּמָגִנָּם הוּא: יִרְאֵי יְיָ בִּטְחוּ בַיְיָ, עֶזְרָם וּמָגִנָּם הוּא:

יְיָ זְכָרָנוּ יְבָרֵךְ, יְבָרֵךְ אֶת־בֵּית יִשְׂרָאֵל. יְבָרֵךְ אֶת־בֵּית אַהֲרֹן: יְבָרֵךְ יִרְאֵי יְיָ, הַקְּטַנִּים עִם־הַגְּדֹלִים: יֹסֵף יְיָ עֲלֵיכֶם, עֲלֵיכֶם וְעַל־בְּנֵיכֶם: בְּרוּכִים אַתֶּם לַיְיָ, עֹשֵׂה שָׁמַיִם וָאָרֶץ: הַשָּׁמַיִם שָׁמַיִם לַיְיָ, וְהָאָרֶץ נָתַן לִבְנֵי־אָדָם: לֹא־הַמֵּתִים יְהַלְלוּ־יָהּ, וְלֹא כָּל־יֹרְדֵי דוּמָה: וַאֲנַחְנוּ נְבָרֵךְ יָהּ, מֵעַתָּה וְעַד־עוֹלָם הַלְלוּיָהּ:

of the world depends upon a time "when the knowledge of the Lord will cover the world as the waters cover the sea" (Is. 11:9). בַּיוֹם הַהוּא יִהְיֶה ה' אֶחָד וּשְׁמוֹ אֶחָד, "In that day the Lord will be one and His Name one" (Zech. 14:9), because everyone will recognize Him. This will be the world of true peace for which we all pray at the conclusion of the Seder. This is the hope and message of the fifth cup.

HALLEL

PSALMS OF PRAISE

The fourth cup is filled.

Not unto us, O Eternal, not unto us, but unto Thyself give glory, for Thy mercy and Thy truth. Wherefore should the nations say, "Where, now, is their God?" Our God is in heaven and He does what He wills. Their idols are silver or gold, the work of human hands. They have a mouth but speak not; they have eyes but see not; they have ears but hear not; they have a nose but smell not; they have hands but feel not; they have feet but walk not; they make no sound in their throat; Like them are those who make them and those who trust in them. Let Israel trust in the Eternal; He is their help and shield. Let the house of Aaron trust in the Eternal; He is their help and shield. Let those who revere the Eternal trust in the Eternal; He is their help and shield.

The Eternal has been mindful of us; He will bless the house of Israel and the house of Aaron. He will bless those who revere the Eternal, the lowly and the great. May the Eternal increase you and your children. Blessed are you of the Eternal, the Maker of the heaven and earth. The heavens are the heavens of the Eternal, and the earth He has given to the children of men. The dead praise not the Eternal, nor all who go down to silence. But we will bless the Eternal, henceforth and forever. Halleluyah— Praise the Eternal.

אָהַבְתִּי כִּי־יִשְׁמַע יְיָ, אֶת־קוֹלִי תַּחֲנוּנָי: כִּי־הִטָּה אָזְנוֹ לִי, וּבְיָמַי אֶקְרָא:
אֲפָפוּנִי חֶבְלֵי־מָוֶת, וּמְצָרֵי שְׁאוֹל מְצָאוּנִי, צָרָה וְיָגוֹן אֶמְצָא: וּבְשֵׁם־יְיָ
אֶקְרָא, אָנָּה יְיָ מַלְּטָה נַפְשִׁי: חַנּוּן יְיָ וְצַדִּיק, וֵאלֹהֵינוּ מְרַחֵם: שֹׁמֵר
פְּתָאיִם יְיָ, דַּלּוֹתִי וְלִי יְהוֹשִׁיעַ: שׁוּבִי נַפְשִׁי לִמְנוּחָיְכִי, כִּי יְיָ גָּמַל
עָלָיְכִי: כִּי חִלַּצְתָּ נַפְשִׁי מִמָּוֶת, אֶת־עֵינִי מִן־דִּמְעָה, אֶת־רַגְלִי מִדֶּחִי:
אֶתְהַלֵּךְ לִפְנֵי יְיָ, בְּאַרְצוֹת הַחַיִּים: הֶאֱמַנְתִּי כִּי אֲדַבֵּר, אֲנִי עָנִיתִי מְאֹד:
אֲנִי אָמַרְתִּי בְחָפְזִי, כָּל־הָאָדָם כֹּזֵב:

מָה־אָשִׁיב לַיְיָ, כָּל־תַּגְמוּלוֹהִי עָלָי: כּוֹס־יְשׁוּעוֹת אֶשָּׂא, וּבְשֵׁם יְיָ
אֶקְרָא: נְדָרַי לַיְיָ אֲשַׁלֵּם, נֶגְדָה־נָּא לְכָל־עַמּוֹ: יָקָר בְּעֵינֵי יְיָ, הַמָּוְתָה
לַחֲסִידָיו: אָנָּה יְיָ כִּי־אֲנִי עַבְדֶּךָ, אֲנִי עַבְדְּךָ בֶּן־אֲמָתֶךָ, פִּתַּחְתָּ לְמוֹסֵרָי:
לְךָ אֶזְבַּח זֶבַח תּוֹדָה, וּבְשֵׁם יְיָ אֶקְרָא: נְדָרַי לַיְיָ אֲשַׁלֵּם, נֶגְדָה־נָּא לְכָל־
עַמּוֹ: בְּחַצְרוֹת בֵּית יְיָ, בְּתוֹכֵכִי יְרוּשָׁלָיִם, הַלְלוּיָהּ:

הַלְלוּ אֶת־יְיָ כָּל־גּוֹיִם, שַׁבְּחוּהוּ כָּל־הָאֻמִּים: כִּי גָבַר עָלֵינוּ חַסְדּוֹ,
וֶאֱמֶת־יְיָ לְעוֹלָם, הַלְלוּיָהּ:

כִּי לְעוֹלָם חַסְדּוֹ:	הוֹדוּ לַיְיָ כִּי־טוֹב.
כִּי לְעוֹלָם חַסְדּוֹ:	יֹאמַר־נָא יִשְׂרָאֵל.
כִּי לְעוֹלָם חַסְדּוֹ:	יֹאמְרוּ־נָא בֵית־אַהֲרֹן.
כִּי לְעוֹלָם חַסְדּוֹ:	יֹאמְרוּ־נָא יִרְאֵי יְיָ.

I love the Eternal, for He has heard my voice and my supplications. Because He has inclined His ear to me, I will call upon Him all my days. The struggles of death encompassed me, the agony of the grave seized me, trouble and sorrow met me. But I called upon the name of the Eternal, "Eternal, I beseech Thee, save me." Gracious is the Eternal and righteous; our God is merciful. The Eternal watches over the simple; I was brought low and He saved me. Be at rest again, O my soul, for the Eternal has dealt bountifully with thee; for He has saved me from death, my eyes from tears and my foot from stumbling. I shall yet walk before the Eternal in the lands of the living. I had faith even when I said, "I am greatly afflicted." Only in my haste did I say: "All men are deceitful."

What can I render unto the Eternal for all His benefactions to me? I will lift up the cup of salvation, and proclaim the name of the Eternal. My vows unto the Eternal I will fulfill; would it were in the presence of all His people! Costly in the eyes of the Eternal is the death of His pious servants. I pray, O Eternal, for I am Thy servant, I, Thy servant, child of Thy handmaid; Thou hast loosed my bonds. To Thee I will offer thanksgiving sacrifice, and call on the name of the Eternal. My vows to the Eternal I will fulfill; would it were in the presence of all His people, in the courts of the Eternal, in the midst of thee, O Jerusalem! Halleluyah—Praise the Eternal.

Praise the Eternal, all nations, laud Him, all peoples, for great is His mercy toward us, and the faithfulness of the Eternal is forever. Halleluyah—Praise the Eternal.

Give thanks to the Eternal, for He is good; His mercy endures forever. Let Israel say: His mercy endures forever. Let the house of Aaron say: His mercy endures forever. Let those who revere the Eternal say: His mercy endures forever.

מִן־הַמֵּצַר קָרָאתִי יָּהּ, עָנָנִי בַמֶּרְחַב יָהּ: יְיָ לִי לֹא אִירָא, מַה־יַּעֲשֶׂה לִי אָדָם: יְיָ לִי בְּעֹזְרָי. וַאֲנִי אֶרְאֶה בְשֹׂנְאָי: טוֹב לַחֲסוֹת בַּיְיָ, מִבְּטֹחַ בָּאָדָם: טוֹב לַחֲסוֹת בַּיְיָ. מִבְּטֹחַ בִּנְדִיבִים: כָּל־גּוֹיִם סְבָבוּנִי, בְּשֵׁם יְיָ כִּי אֲמִילַם: סַבּוּנִי גַם־סְבָבוּנִי, בְּשֵׁם יְיָ כִּי אֲמִילַם: סַבּוּנִי כִדְבֹרִים, דֹּעֲכוּ כְּאֵשׁ קוֹצִים, בְּשֵׁם יְיָ כִּי אֲמִילַם: דָּחֹה דְחִיתַנִי לִנְפֹּל, וַיְיָ עֲזָרָנִי: עָזִּי וְזִמְרָת יָהּ, וַיְהִי־לִי לִישׁוּעָה: קוֹל רִנָּה וִישׁוּעָה, בְּאָהֳלֵי צַדִּיקִים, יְמִין יְיָ עֹשָׂה חָיִל: יְמִין יְיָ רוֹמֵמָה, יְמִין יְיָ עֹשָׂה חָיִל: לֹא אָמוּת כִּי אֶחְיֶה, וַאֲסַפֵּר מַעֲשֵׂי יָהּ: יַסֹּר יִסְּרַנִי יָּהּ, וְלַמָּוֶת לֹא נְתָנָנִי: פִּתְחוּ־לִי שַׁעֲרֵי־צֶדֶק, אָבֹא־בָם אוֹדֶה יָהּ: זֶה־הַשַּׁעַר לַיְיָ, צַדִּיקִים יָבֹאוּ בוֹ: אוֹדְךָ כִּי עֲנִיתָנִי, וַתְּהִי־לִי לִישׁוּעָה: אוֹדְךָ כִּי עֲנִיתָנִי, וַתְּהִי־לִי לִישׁוּעָה: אֶבֶן מָאֲסוּ הַבּוֹנִים, הָיְתָה לְרֹאשׁ פִּנָּה: אֶבֶן מָאֲסוּ הַבּוֹנִים, הָיְתָה לְרֹאשׁ פִּנָּה: מֵאֵת יְיָ הָיְתָה זֹּאת, הִיא נִפְלָאת בְּעֵינֵינוּ: מֵאֵת יְיָ הָיְתָה זֹּאת, הִיא נִפְלָאת בְּעֵינֵינוּ: זֶה־הַיּוֹם עָשָׂה יְיָ, נָגִילָה וְנִשְׂמְחָה בוֹ: זֶה־הַיּוֹם עָשָׂה יְיָ, נָגִילָה וְנִשְׂמְחָה בוֹ:

אָנָּא יְיָ הוֹשִׁיעָה נָּא: אָנָּא יְיָ הוֹשִׁיעָה נָּא:

אָנָּא יְיָ הַצְלִיחָה נָא: אָנָּא יְיָ הַצְלִיחָה נָא:

בָּרוּךְ הַבָּא בְּשֵׁם יְיָ, בֵּרַכְנוּכֶם מִבֵּית יְיָ: בָּרוּךְ הַבָּא בְּשֵׁם יְיָ, בֵּרַכְנוּכֶם מִבֵּית יְיָ: אֵל יְיָ וַיָּאֶר לָנוּ, אִסְרוּ־חַג בַּעֲבֹתִים, עַד־קַרְנוֹת הַמִּזְבֵּחַ: אֵל יְיָ וַיָּאֶר לָנוּ, אִסְרוּ־חַג בַּעֲבֹתִים, עַד־קַרְנוֹת הַמִּזְבֵּחַ: אֵלִי אַתָּה וְאוֹדֶךָּ,

Out of my straits I called upon the Eternal; He answered me by setting me free. The Eternal is for me, I shall not fear. What can man do unto me? The Eternal is my helper and I shall see victory over my enemies. It is better to trust in the Eternal than to rely on man. It is better to trust in the Eternal than to rely on princes. The nations beset me; in the name of the Eternal I will surely cut them down. They surround me, yea, they encompass me; in the name of the Eternal I will surely cut them down. They encompass me about like bees; they will be quenched as a fire of thorns; in the name of the Eternal I will surely cut them down. They thrust at me that I might fall, but the Eternal supports me. The Eternal is my strength and song, He has become my salvation. Hark, the joyous song of victory is heard in the tents of the righteous; the right hand of the Eternal does valiantly. The right hand of the Eternal is exalted; the right hand of the Eternal does valiantly. I shall not die, but live and declare the works of the Eternal. Though the Eternal has indeed chastened me, He has not given me over to death. Open to me the gates of righteousness, I will enter them to praise the Eternal. This is the gate of the Eternal, the righteous shall enter it. I will give thanks unto Thee, for Thou hast answered me, and become my salvation. I will give thanks unto Thee, for Thou hast answered me, and become my salvation. The stone which the builders rejected has become the cornerstone. The stone which the builders rejected has become the cornerstone. This is the work of the Eternal; it is marvelous in our eyes. This is the work of the Eternal; it is marvelous in our eyes. This is the day the Eternal has made; let us rejoice and be glad in it. This is the day the Eternal has made; let us rejoice and be glad in it.

Eternal, we beseech Thee, save us. Eternal, we beseech Thee, save us. Eternal, we beseech Thee, prosper us. Eternal, we beseech Thee, prosper us.

Blessed be you who come in the name of the Eternal; we bless you from the house of the Eternal. Blessed be you who come in the name of the Eternal; we bless you from the house of the Eternal. The Eternal is God and has given us light; bring the sacrifice bound with myrtle to the very horns of the altar. The Eternal is

אֱלֹהַי אֲרוֹמְמֶךָּ: אֵלִי אַתָּה וְאוֹדֶךָּ, אֱלֹהַי אֲרוֹמְמֶךָּ: הוֹדוּ לַיְיָ כִּי־טוֹב, כִּי
לְעוֹלָם חַסְדּוֹ: הוֹדוּ לַיְיָ כִּי־טוֹב, כִּי לְעוֹלָם חַסְדּוֹ:

כִּי לְעוֹלָם חַסְדּוֹ:	הוֹדוּ לַיְיָ כִּי־טוֹב,
כִּי לְעוֹלָם חַסְדּוֹ:	הוֹדוּ לֵאלֹהֵי הָאֱלֹהִים,
כִּי לְעוֹלָם חַסְדּוֹ:	הוֹדוּ לַאֲדֹנֵי הָאֲדֹנִים,
כִּי לְעוֹלָם חַסְדּוֹ:	לְעֹשֵׂה נִפְלָאוֹת גְּדֹלוֹת לְבַדּוֹ,
כִּי לְעוֹלָם חַסְדּוֹ:	לְעֹשֵׂה הַשָּׁמַיִם בִּתְבוּנָה,
כִּי לְעוֹלָם חַסְדּוֹ:	לְרוֹקַע הָאָרֶץ עַל־הַמָּיִם,
כִּי לְעוֹלָם חַסְדּוֹ:	לְעֹשֵׂה אוֹרִים גְּדֹלִים,
כִּי לְעוֹלָם חַסְדּוֹ:	אֶת־הַשֶּׁמֶשׁ לְמֶמְשֶׁלֶת בַּיּוֹם,
כִּי לְעוֹלָם חַסְדּוֹ:	אֶת־הַיָּרֵחַ וְכוֹכָבִים לְמֶמְשְׁלוֹת בַּלָּיְלָה,
כִּי לְעוֹלָם חַסְדּוֹ:	לְמַכֵּה מִצְרַיִם בִּבְכוֹרֵיהֶם,
כִּי לְעוֹלָם חַסְדּוֹ:	וַיּוֹצֵא יִשְׂרָאֵל מִתּוֹכָם,
כִּי לְעוֹלָם חַסְדּוֹ:	בְּיָד חֲזָקָה וּבִזְרוֹעַ נְטוּיָה,
כִּי לְעוֹלָם חַסְדּוֹ:	לְגֹזֵר יַם־סוּף לִגְזָרִים,
כִּי לְעוֹלָם חַסְדּוֹ:	וְהֶעֱבִיר יִשְׂרָאֵל בְּתוֹכוֹ,
כִּי לְעוֹלָם חַסְדּוֹ:	וְנִעֵר פַּרְעֹה וְחֵילוֹ בְיַם־סוּף,

God and has given us light; bring the sacrifice bound with myrtle to the very horns of the altar. Thou art my God and I will give thanks unto Thee; my God, I will extol Thee. Thou art my God and I will give thanks unto Thee; my God, I will extol Thee. Give thanks to the Eternal for He is good; His mercy endures forever. Give thanks to the Eternal for He is good; His mercy endures forever.

Give thanks to the Eternal for He is good;
For His mercy endures forever.
Give thanks to the God of gods;
For His mercy endures forever.
Give thanks to the Lord of lords;
For His mercy endures forever.
To Him Who alone performs great miracles;
For His mercy endures forever.
To Him Who made the heavens with wisdom,
For His mercy endures forever.
To Him Who spread the earth above the waters;
For His mercy endures forever.
To Him Who made the great lights
For His mercy endures forever.
The sun to rule by day;
For His mercy endures forever.
The moon and the stars to rule by night;
For His mercy endures forever.
To Him Who smote Egypt through their first-born;
For His mercy endures forever.
And brought Israel forth from among them,
For His mercy endures forever.
With a mighty hand and an outstretched arm;
For His mercy endures forever.
To Him Who divided the Red Sea,
For His mercy endures forever.
And brought Israel through it,
For His mercy endures forever.
Who drowned Pharaoh and his host in the Red Sea;
For His mercy endures forever.

כִּי לְעוֹלָם חַסְדּוֹ:	לְמוֹלִיךְ עַמּוֹ בַּמִּדְבָּר,
כִּי לְעוֹלָם חַסְדּוֹ:	לְמַכֵּה מְלָכִים גְּדֹלִים,
כִּי לְעוֹלָם חַסְדּוֹ:	וַיַּהֲרֹג מְלָכִים אַדִּירִים,
כִּי לְעוֹלָם חַסְדּוֹ:	לְסִיחוֹן מֶלֶךְ הָאֱמֹרִי,
כִּי לְעוֹלָם חַסְדּוֹ:	וּלְעוֹג מֶלֶךְ הַבָּשָׁן,
כִּי לְעוֹלָם חַסְדּוֹ:	וְנָתַן אַרְצָם לְנַחֲלָה,
כִּי לְעוֹלָם חַסְדּוֹ:	נַחֲלָה לְיִשְׂרָאֵל עַבְדּוֹ,
כִּי לְעוֹלָם חַסְדּוֹ:	שֶׁבְּשִׁפְלֵנוּ זָכַר־לָנוּ,
כִּי לְעוֹלָם חַסְדּוֹ:	וַיִּפְרְקֵנוּ מִצָּרֵינוּ,
כִּי לְעוֹלָם חַסְדּוֹ:	נֹתֵן לֶחֶם לְכָל־בָּשָׂר,
כִּי לְעוֹלָם חַסְדּוֹ:	הוֹדוּ לְאֵל הַשָּׁמָיִם,

נִשְׁמַת כָּל־חַי תְּבָרֵךְ אֶת־שִׁמְךָ יְיָ אֱלֹהֵינוּ. וְרוּחַ כָּל־בָּשָׂר תְּפָאֵר
וּתְרוֹמֵם זִכְרְךָ מַלְכֵּנוּ תָּמִיד. מִן־הָעוֹלָם וְעַד־הָעוֹלָם אַתָּה אֵל,
וּמִבַּלְעָדֶיךָ אֵין לָנוּ מֶלֶךְ גּוֹאֵל וּמוֹשִׁיעַ. פּוֹדֶה וּמַצִּיל וּמְפַרְנֵס וּמְרַחֵם
בְּכָל־עֵת צָרָה וְצוּקָה. אֵין לָנוּ מֶלֶךְ אֶלָּא אָתָּה: אֱלֹהֵי הָרִאשׁוֹנִים
וְהָאַחֲרוֹנִים אֱלוֹהַּ כָּל־בְּרִיּוֹת, אֲדוֹן כָּל־תּוֹלָדוֹת, הַמְהֻלָּל בְּרֹב
הַתִּשְׁבָּחוֹת, הַמְנַהֵג עוֹלָמוֹ בְּחֶסֶד, וּבְרִיּוֹתָיו בְּרַחֲמִים. וַיְיָ לֹא־יָנוּם וְלֹא
יִישָׁן. הַמְעוֹרֵר יְשֵׁנִים וְהַמֵּקִיץ נִרְדָּמִים וְהַמֵּשִׂיחַ אִלְּמִים וְהַמַּתִּיר
אֲסוּרִים וְהַסּוֹמֵךְ נוֹפְלִים וְהַזּוֹקֵף כְּפוּפִים. לְךָ לְבַדְּךָ אֲנַחְנוּ מוֹדִים:
אִלּוּ פִינוּ מָלֵא שִׁירָה כַיָּם, וּלְשׁוֹנֵנוּ רִנָּה כַּהֲמוֹן גַּלָּיו, וְשִׂפְתוֹתֵינוּ שֶׁבַח
כְּמֶרְחֲבֵי רָקִיעַ, וְעֵינֵינוּ מְאִירוֹת כַּשֶּׁמֶשׁ וְכַיָּרֵחַ, וְיָדֵינוּ פְרוּשׂוֹת כְּנִשְׁרֵי

To Him Who led His people through the wilderness;
For His mercy endures forever.
To Him Who smote great kings,
For His mercy endures forever.
And slew mighty kings;
For His mercy endures forever.
Sihon, king of the Amorites,
For His mercy endures forever.
And Og, king of Bashan,
For His mercy endures forever.
And gave their land as a heritage,
For His mercy endures forever.
A heritage to Israel, His servant;
For His mercy endures forever.
Who remembered us in our lowliness,
For his mercy endures forever.
And redeemed us from those who oppressed us:
For His mercy endures forever.
Who gives food to all;
For His mercy endures forever.
Give thanks to the God of the heavens,
For His mercy endures forever.

The soul of every living being shall bless Your name, Eternal our God; the spirit of all flesh shall ever adore and extol Your fame, our King. From everlasting to everlasting You are God, and besides You we have no Ruler or Deliverer, Redeemer, Sustainer, Who is merciful every time of sorrow and distress; we have no King except You. O God of the beginning and of the end, God of all creatures, Master of all existence, Who is praised in manifold praises, Who leads the world with loving-kindness and His creatures with mercy; God Who neither slumbers nor sleeps, Who awakens the sleeping and stirs the slumbering, gives speech to the dumb and loosens the bound, supports the falling and upholds the bowed-down, to You alone we give thanks. Were our mouths filled with singing as the sea, and our tongue uplifted in song as the waves, and our lips with praise as the spacious firmament,

שָׁמַיִם, וְרַגְלֵינוּ קַלּוֹת כָּאַיָּלוֹת, אֵין אֲנַחְנוּ מַסְפִּיקִים לְהוֹדוֹת לְךָ, יְיָ
אֱלֹהֵינוּ וֵאלֹהֵי אֲבוֹתֵינוּ, וּלְבָרֵךְ אֶת־שְׁמֶךָ, עַל־אַחַת מֵאֶלֶף, אֶלֶף אַלְפֵי
אֲלָפִים וְרִבֵּי רְבָבוֹת פְּעָמִים הַטּוֹבוֹת שֶׁעָשִׂיתָ עִם־אֲבוֹתֵינוּ וְעִמָּנוּ:
מִמִּצְרַיִם גְּאַלְתָּנוּ יְיָ אֱלֹהֵינוּ, וּמִבֵּית עֲבָדִים פְּדִיתָנוּ. בְּרָעָב זַנְתָּנוּ
וּבְשָׂבָע כִּלְכַּלְתָּנוּ, מֵחֶרֶב הִצַּלְתָּנוּ, וּמִדֶּבֶר מִלַּטְתָּנוּ, וּמֵחֳלָיִם רָעִים
וְנֶאֱמָנִים דִּלִּיתָנוּ. עַד־הֵנָּה עֲזָרוּנוּ רַחֲמֶיךָ, וְלֹא־עֲזָבוּנוּ חֲסָדֶיךָ. וְאַל
תִּטְּשֵׁנוּ יְיָ אֱלֹהֵינוּ לָנֶצַח: עַל־כֵּן אֵבָרִים שֶׁפִּלַּגְתָּ בָּנוּ, וְרוּחַ וּנְשָׁמָה
שֶׁנָּפַחְתָּ בְּאַפֵּינוּ, וְלָשׁוֹן אֲשֶׁר שַׂמְתָּ בְּפִינוּ, הֵן הֵם יוֹדוּ וִיבָרְכוּ וִישַׁבְּחוּ
וִיפָאֲרוּ וִירוֹמְמוּ וְיַעֲרִיצוּ וְיַקְדִּישׁוּ וְיַמְלִיכוּ אֶת־שִׁמְךָ מַלְכֵּנוּ: כִּי
כָל־פֶּה לְךָ יוֹדֶה, וְכָל־לָשׁוֹן לְךָ תִשָּׁבַע, וְכָל־בֶּרֶךְ לְךָ תִכְרַע, וְכָל־קוֹמָה
לְפָנֶיךָ תִשְׁתַּחֲוֶה. וְכָל־לְבָבוֹת יִירָאוּךָ וְכָל־קֶרֶב וּכְלָיוֹת יְזַמְּרוּ לִשְׁמֶךָ,
כַּדָּבָר שֶׁכָּתוּב: כָּל־עַצְמוֹתַי תֹּאמַרְנָה יְיָ מִי כָמוֹךָ: מַצִּיל עָנִי מֵחָזָק
מִמֶּנּוּ וְעָנִי וְאֶבְיוֹן מִגֹּזְלוֹ: מִי יִדְמֶה־לָּךְ, וּמִי יִשְׁוֶה־לָּךְ, וּמִי יַעֲרָךְ־לָךְ.
הָאֵל הַגָּדוֹל הַגִּבּוֹר וְהַנּוֹרָא אֵל עֶלְיוֹן, קֹנֵה שָׁמַיִם וָאָרֶץ: נְהַלֶּלְךָ
וּנְשַׁבֵּחֲךָ וּנְפָאֶרְךָ וּנְבָרֵךְ אֶת־שֵׁם קָדְשֶׁךָ כָּאָמוּר: לְדָוִד בָּרְכִי נַפְשִׁי
אֶת־יְיָ וְכָל־קְרָבַי אֶת־שֵׁם קָדְשׁוֹ:

הָאֵל בְּתַעֲצֻמוֹת עֻזֶּךָ, הַגָּדוֹל בִּכְבוֹד שְׁמֶךָ הַגִּבּוֹר לָנֶצַח וְהַנּוֹרָא
בְּנוֹרְאוֹתֶיךָ. הַמֶּלֶךְ הַיּוֹשֵׁב עַל־כִּסֵּא רָם וְנִשָּׂא:

שׁוֹכֵן־עַד, מָרוֹם וְקָדוֹשׁ שְׁמוֹ: וְכָתוּב: רַנְּנוּ צַדִּיקִים בַּיְיָ לַיְשָׁרִים נָאוָה
תְהִלָּה:

and our eyes shining as the sun and the moon, and our hands stretched out as the eagles of the skies, and our feet swift as the hinds, we would still not be able to offer proper thanks to You, Eternal our God and God of our fathers, and to praise Your Name one thousandth share or even a tenth of one thousandth share for the manifold goodness You bestowed upon our forefathers and upon us. From Egypt You redeemed us, O Eternal our God, and from the house of bondage You liberated us. In famine You fed us, in plenty You sustained us, from the sword You saved us, from pestilence You delivered us, from severe sickness You spared us. Heretofore Your mercy helped us and Your loving-kindness did not forsake us. Do not forsake us evermore, we pray You, Eternal our God. Therefore, the limbs You have fashioned within us, and the spirit of life which You have breathed into us, and the tongue which You have placed in our mouth, they shall all thank, praise, extol, glorify, exalt, adore, hallow, and give sovereignty to Your name, for every mouth shall give thanks to You, and every tongue shall pledge fealty to You; and every knee shall bend to You, and every living being shall bow down to You; all hearts shall revere You, and all inner parts shall sing to Your Name, as it is written: "All my bones shall say, Eternal, who is like unto Thee, delivering the afflicted from one stronger than he, and the needy from one who would rob him!" Who is like unto You, and who can equal You? Who can compare with You, O God, great, mighty, revered, supreme God, Master of heaven and earth? Let us praise and worship, glorify and bless Your holy Name, as it is said by David: "O my soul, bless the Eternal, and all that is within me, bless His holy Name."

You are God by the power of Your might, great by the glory of Your Name, almighty forever and inspiring awe by Your deeds. You are the Ruler enthroned sublimely and exalted.

You Who dwell in eternity, exalted and holy is Your Name. And it is written: "Rejoice in the Eternal, ye righteous, for it becometh the upright to speak His praise."

בְּפִי יְשָׁרִים תִּתְהַלָּל, וּבְדִבְרֵי צַדִּיקִים תִּתְבָּרַךְ, וּבִלְשׁוֹן חֲסִידִים תִּתְרוֹמָם, וּבְקֶרֶב קְדוֹשִׁים תִּתְקַדָּשׁ:

וּבְמַקְהֲלוֹת רִבְבוֹת עַמְּךָ בֵּית יִשְׂרָאֵל בְּרִנָּה יִתְפָּאַר שִׁמְךָ, מַלְכֵּנוּ, בְּכָל־דּוֹר וָדוֹר. שֶׁכֵּן חוֹבַת כָּל־הַיְצוּרִים. לְפָנֶיךָ יְיָ אֱלֹהֵינוּ וֵאלֹהֵי אֲבוֹתֵינוּ, לְהוֹדוֹת, לְהַלֵּל, לְשַׁבֵּחַ, לְפָאֵר, לְרוֹמֵם, לְהַדֵּר, לְבָרֵךְ, לְעַלֵּה וּלְקַלֵּס, עַל כָּל־דִּבְרֵי שִׁירוֹת וְתִשְׁבְּחוֹת דָּוִד בֶּן־יִשַׁי עַבְדְּךָ מְשִׁיחֶךָ:

יִשְׁתַּבַּח שִׁמְךָ לָעַד מַלְכֵּנוּ. הָאֵל הַמֶּלֶךְ הַגָּדוֹל וְהַקָּדוֹשׁ בַּשָּׁמַיִם וּבָאָרֶץ. כִּי־לְךָ נָאֶה יְיָ אֱלֹהֵינוּ וֵאלֹהֵי אֲבוֹתֵינוּ, שִׁיר וּשְׁבָחָה, הַלֵּל וְזִמְרָה, עֹז וּמֶמְשָׁלָה, נֶצַח, גְּדֻלָּה וּגְבוּרָה, תְּהִלָּה וְתִפְאֶרֶת, קְדֻשָּׁה וּמַלְכוּת, בְּרָכוֹת וְהוֹדָאוֹת, מֵעַתָּה וְעַד־עוֹלָם:

יְהַלְלוּךָ יְיָ אֱלֹהֵינוּ כָּל־מַעֲשֶׂיךָ וַחֲסִידֶיךָ צַדִּיקִים עוֹשֵׂי רְצוֹנֶךָ. וְכָל־עַמְּךָ בֵּית יִשְׂרָאֵל בְּרִנָּה יוֹדוּ, וִיבָרְכוּ, וִישַׁבְּחוּ, וִיפָאֲרוּ וִירוֹמְמוּ, וְיַעֲרִיצוּ וְיַקְדִּישׁוּ, וְיַמְלִיכוּ אֶת־שִׁמְךָ מַלְכֵּנוּ. כִּי־לְךָ טוֹב לְהוֹדוֹת וּלְשִׁמְךָ נָאֶה לְזַמֵּר, כִּי מֵעוֹלָם וְעַד־עוֹלָם אַתָּה אֵל: בָּרוּךְ אַתָּה יְיָ, מֶלֶךְ מְהֻלָּל בַּתִּשְׁבָּחוֹת:

כּוֹס רְבִיעִית

הִנְנִי מוּכָן וּמְזֻמָּן לְקַיֵּם מִצְוַת כּוֹס רְבִיעִית מֵאַרְבַּע כּוֹסוֹת לְשֵׁם יִחוּד קֻדְשָׁא בְּרִיךְ־הוּא וּשְׁכִינְתֵּיהּ עַל־יְדֵי הַהוּא טָמִיר וְנֶעְלָם בְּשֵׁם כָּל־יִשְׂרָאֵל.

בָּרוּךְ אַתָּה יְיָ, אֱלֹהֵינוּ מֶלֶךְ הָעוֹלָם, בּוֹרֵא פְּרִי הַגָּפֶן:

Drink the entire fourth cup of wine while leaning to the left.

By the mouth of the upright You shall be lauded, and by the words of the righteous You shall be praised; by the tongue of the pious You shall be exalted, and in the midst of the holy You shall be hallowed.

In the assemblies of the multitudes of Your people, the House of Israel, Your name, O our Ruler, shall be glorified with song in every generation. For it is the duty of all creatures to give thanks, to praise, to exalt, to bless, to adore, and to extol You, O Eternal our God, and the God of our fathers, in the words of the songs and psalms of David the son of Jesse, Your anointed servant.

Praised be Your name forever, our Ruler, O God, Who rules and is great and holy in the heavens and on the earth; for to You, Eternal our God and God of our fathers, it is befitting to render song and praise, prayer and psalms, expressing strength and rule, victory, glory and might, praise and beauty, holiness and sovereignty, blessings and thanksgivings, from now and forever.

All Thy works, O Eternal, shall praise Thee; Thy pious servants, the righteous who do Thy will, indeed all Thy people the House of Israel, with joyful song shall give thanks, bless, praise, glorify, extol, revere, sanctify and enthrone Thy name, O our King, for unto Thee it is good to give thanks, and unto Thy name it is proper to sing praises, for Thou art God from everlasting to everlasting. Blessed art Thou, Eternal, King extolled in praises.

THE FOURTH CUP

Blessed art Thou, Eternal our God, Ruler of the universe, Creator of the fruit of the vine.

Drink the entire fourth cup of wine while leaning to the left.

בָּרוּךְ אַתָּה יְיָ, אֱלֹהֵינוּ מֶלֶךְ הָעוֹלָם, עַל הַגֶּפֶן וְעַל פְּרִי הַגֶּפֶן, וְעַל
תְּנוּבַת הַשָּׂדֶה, וְעַל אֶרֶץ חֶמְדָּה טוֹבָה וּרְחָבָה, שֶׁרָצִיתָ וְהִנְחַלְתָּ
לַאֲבוֹתֵינוּ, לֶאֱכוֹל מִפִּרְיָהּ וְלִשְׂבּוֹעַ מִטּוּבָהּ. רַחֶם נָא יְיָ אֱלֹהֵינוּ עַל
יִשְׂרָאֵל עַמֶּךָ, וְעַל יְרוּשָׁלַיִם עִירֶךָ, וְעַל צִיּוֹן מִשְׁכַּן כְּבוֹדֶךָ, וְעַל מִזְבְּחֶךָ
וְעַל הֵיכָלֶךָ. וּבְנֵה יְרוּשָׁלַיִם עִיר הַקֹּדֶשׁ בִּמְהֵרָה בְיָמֵינוּ, וְהַעֲלֵנוּ
לְתוֹכָהּ, וְשַׂמְּחֵנוּ בְּבִנְיָנָהּ, וְנֹאכַל מִפִּרְיָהּ, וְנִשְׂבַּע מִטּוּבָהּ, וּנְבָרֶכְךָ עָלֶיהָ
בִּקְדֻשָּׁה וּבְטָהֳרָה: (בשבת וּרְצֵה וְהַחֲלִיצֵנוּ בְּיוֹם הַשַּׁבָּת הַזֶּה) וְשַׂמְּחֵנוּ
בְּיוֹם חַג הַמַּצּוֹת הַזֶּה: כִּי אַתָּה יְיָ טוֹב וּמֵטִיב לַכֹּל וְנוֹדֶה־לְּךָ עַל הָאָרֶץ
וְעַל פְּרִי הַגֶּפֶן: בָּרוּךְ אַתָּה יְיָ, עַל הָאָרֶץ וְעַל פְּרִי הַגֶּפֶן:

נִרְצָה

חֲסַל סִדּוּר פֶּסַח כְּהִלְכָתוֹ. כְּכָל מִשְׁפָּטוֹ וְחֻקָּתוֹ. כַּאֲשֶׁר זָכִינוּ, לְסַדֵּר
אוֹתוֹ, כֵּן נִזְכֶּה לַעֲשׂוֹתוֹ: זָךְ שׁוֹכֵן מְעוֹנָה. קוֹמֵם קְהַל עֲדַת מִי מָנָה.
בְּקָרוֹב נַהֵל, נִטְעֵי כַנָּה פְּדוּיִם לְצִיּוֹן בְּרִנָּה:

לְשָׁנָה הַבָּאָה בִּירוּשָׁלָיִם:

Blessed art Thou, Eternal our God, Ruler of the universe, for the vine, and for the fruit of the vine, for the produce of the field and for that precious, good and spacious land which You gave to our ancestors, to eat of its fruit, and to enjoy its goodness. Have compassion, O Eternal our God, upon us, upon Israel Your people, upon Jerusalem Your city, on Zion the abode of Your glory, and upon Your altar and Your Temple. Rebuild Jerusalem, Your holy city, speedily in our days. Bring us there, and cheer us with her rebuilding; may we eat of her fruit and enjoy her blessings; and we will bless You for this in holiness and purity. (*On the Sabbath add*: Be gracious to us and give us strength on this Sabbath day.) Grant us joy on this Festival of Matzoth, for You, O God, are good and beneficent to all; and we therefore give thanks unto You for the land and the fruit of the vine. Blessed art Thou, Eternal, for the land and the fruit of the vine.

NIRTZAH

CONCLUSION OF THE SEDER

Ended is the Passover Seder
  According to custom, statute and law.
As we were worthy to celebrate it this year,
  So may we perform it in future years.
O Pure One in heaven above,
  Restore the congregation of Israel in Your love.
Speedily lead Your redeemed people
  To Zion in joy.

NEXT YEAR IN JERUSALEM

Messianic Redemption

The theme of messianic redemption resonates throughout the Seder but is loudest at the very end. The final clarion call of לְשָׁנָה הַבָּאָה בִּירוּשָׁלַיִם, "Next year in Jerusalem," is the final, formal statement we make at the Seder. This is followed by the recitation of songs and poems, the greatest and most inspiring of which is the Song of Songs, which is recited by many at the conclusion of the Seder.

In this beautiful poem of God's love for Israel, the Almighty addresses us as a lover his beloved. קוֹל דּוֹדִי דוֹפֵק (Song of Songs 5:2)—My Lover knocks hesitantly yet audibly and hopefully. He is anxiously waiting for us to open the door to Him. His knock indicates that He is ever so near to us. It was heard in the War of Independence, in which a small group of Jewish fighters won against incredible odds over hordes of Arabs, and again in the Six-Day War, when our holy city of Jerusalem was liberated. But we have not yet opened the door to Him. We are too comfortable in our palatial surroundings. פָּשַׁטְתִּי אֶת כֻּתָּנְתִּי אֵיכָכָה אֶלְבָּשֶׁנָּה רָחַצְתִּי אֶת רַגְלַי אֵיכָכָה אֲטַנְּפֵם "I have taken off my coat; how shall I put it on? I have washed my feet; how shall I soil them?" (v. 4). We are unwilling to give up the luxuries of the *golah* and move to an unknown land. We should not wait too long. פָּתַחְתִּי אֲנִי לְדוֹדִי וְדוֹדִי חָמַק עָבָר . . . בִּקַּשְׁתִּיהוּ וְלֹא מְצָאתִיהוּ קְרָאתִיו וְלֹא עָנָנִי "I opened the door to

On the first Seder night:

וּבְכֵן וַיְהִי בַּחֲצִי הַלַּיְלָה:

אָז רוֹב־נִסִּים הִפְלֵאתָ בַּלַּיְלָה. בְּרֹאשׁ אַשְׁמֹרֶת זֶה הַלַּיְלָה. גֵּר־צֶדֶק נִצַּחְתּוֹ כְּנֶחֱלַק לוֹ לַיְלָה. וַיְהִי בַּחֲצִי הַלַּיְלָה:

דַּנְתָּ מֶלֶךְ גְּרָר בַּחֲלוֹם הַלַּיְלָה. הִפְחַדְתָּ אֲרַמִּי בְּאֶמֶשׁ לַיְלָה. וַיָּשַׂר יִשְׂרָאֵל לְמַלְאָךְ וַיּוּכַל־לוֹ לַיְלָה. וַיְהִי בַּחֲצִי הַלַּיְלָה:

my Lover but He had gone . . . I sought Him but could not find Him; I called Him but He did not answer" (v. 6).

God will ultimately redeem us, but we can cause the redemption to come sooner. "I the Lord will hasten it [the redemption] in its time" (Isa. 60:22). How, asks the Talmud, can God hasten it if it will come in its time? זָכוּ אֲחִישֶׁנָּה לֹא זָכוּ בְּעִתָּה comes the answer. If they merit it, I will hasten it; if they do not merit it, it will come in its time (*Sanhedrin* 98a).

I am reminded of what happened to me on one of my trips to Mea Shearim, in Jerusalem. There I met a very religious and mystical-minded man named Reb Shemuel, the owner of a shop, who abstained from speech as much as he did from food. When I visited him in his store, he gave me an unexpectedly warm greeting and even spoke a few sentences. When I asked him what caused his sudden happiness and unusual loquacity, he turned to me and said, "The *Mashiah* is in Jerusalem." I smiled, but despite my skepticism, I went to the *kotel* and prayed with special fervor. I listened to the news that night, not expecting but almost hoping to hear a message about the Messiah. The Sabbath came and went. On Sunday, just before departing for New York, I called on Reb Shemuel. "You told me that the Messiah is in Jerusalem," I said. "I waited in vain." Reb Shemuel looked at me very seriously and said, "You are making a great mistake. You think *we* are waiting for *Mashiah*. No, my good friend. The *Mashiah* is waiting for us."

On the first Seder night:

AND THUS IT HAPPENED AT MIDNIGHT!

Of old, most of the wonders You did perform at night.
At the head of the watches is this very night.
Full victory came to Abraham when he divided his company that
night.
IT HAPPENED AT MIDNIGHT!

You judged the king of Gerar in a dream at night;
You frightened Laban in the midst of the night;
And Israel wrestled with God and prevailed at night.
IT HAPPENED AT MIDNIGHT!

זֶרַע בְּכוֹרֵי פַתְרוֹס מָחַצְתָּ בַּחֲצִי הַלַּיְלָה. חֵילָם לֹא מָצְאוּ בְּקוּמָם בַּלַּיְלָה. טִיסַת נְגִיד חֲרֹשֶׁת סִלִּיתָ בְּכוֹכְבֵי לַיְלָה.   וַיְהִי בַּחֲצִי הַלַּיְלָה:

יָעַץ מְחָרֵף לְנוֹפֵף אִוּוּי הוֹבַשְׁתָּ פְגָרָיו בַּלַּיְלָה. כָּרַע בֵּל וּמַצָּבוֹ בְּאִישׁוֹן־לַיְלָה. לְאִישׁ חֲמוּדוֹת נִגְלָה רָז חֲזוֹת־לַיְלָה.   וַיְהִי בַּחֲצִי הַלַּיְלָה:

מִשְׁתַּכֵּר בִּכְלֵי־קֹדֶשׁ נֶהֱרַג בּוֹ בַּלַּיְלָה. נוֹשַׁע מִבּוֹר־אֲרָיוֹת פּוֹתֵר בְּעֲתוּתֵי־לַיְלָה. שִׂנְאָה נָטַר אֲגָגִי וְכָתַב סְפָרִים בַּלַּיְלָה.   וַיְהִי בַּחֲצִי הַלַּיְלָה:

עוֹרַרְתָּ נִצְחֲךָ עָלָיו בְּנֶדֶד שְׁנַת לַיְלָה. פּוּרָה תִדְרוֹךְ לְשׁוֹמֵר מַה מִּלַּיְלָה. צָרַח כַּשּׁוֹמֵר וְשָׂח אָתָא בֹקֶר וְגַם לָיְלָה.   וַיְהִי בַּחֲצִי הַלַּיְלָה:

קָרֵב יוֹם, אֲשֶׁר הוּא לֹא יוֹם וְלֹא לַיְלָה. רָם הוֹדַע כִּי־לְךָ הַיּוֹם אַף לְךָ הַלַּיְלָה. שׁוֹמְרִים הַפְקֵד לְעִירְךָ כָּל־הַיּוֹם וְכָל־הַלַּיְלָה. תָּאִיר כְּאוֹר־יוֹם חֶשְׁכַּת־לַיְלָה.   וַיְהִי בַּחֲצִי הַלַּיְלָה:

On the second Seder night:

וּבְכֵן וַאֲמַרְתֶּם זֶבַח פֶּסַח:

אֹמֶץ גְּבוּרוֹתֶיךָ הִפְלֵאתָ בַּפֶּסַח. בְּרֹאשׁ כָּל־מוֹעֲדוֹת נִשֵּׂאתָ פֶּסַח. גִּלִּיתָ לְאֶזְרָחִי חֲצוֹת לֵיל־פֶּסַח.   וַאֲמַרְתֶּם זֶבַח פֶּסַח:

You struck down the first-born of Egypt at midnight;
And terrified Midian with a loaf of bread in a dream at night;
The armies of Sisera You swept away by the stars of the night.
IT HAPPENED AT MIDNIGHT!

The Assyrian armies besieging Jerusalem were stricken at night;
Bel and his pedestal were overthrown in the darkness of night;
To Daniel you revealed Your mysteries at night.
IT HAPPENED AT MIDNIGHT!

King Belshazzar of Babylon, become drunk of the holy vessels,
was slain at night;
Daniel, saved from the lion's den, interpreted
the terrifying dreams of the night;
Haman wrote his edicts of hate at night.
IT HAPPENED AT MIDNIGHT!

You achieved Your victory over him in the sleeplessness
of Ahasuerus at night;
You will tread the winepress for them that ask:
"Watchman, what of the night?"
Like the watchman, may he cry out:
"The morning has come even as the night."
IT HAPPENED AT MIDNIGHT!

May the day draw near which is neither day nor night.
O God, make known that Yours is the day and also the night.
Appoint guards over Your city all day and all night.
Make bright like the light of day the darkness of the night.
IT HAPPENED AT MIDNIGHT!

On the second Seder night:

THIS IS THE PASSOVER FESTIVAL!

Your mighty power You did reveal on Passover.
Above all festivals You did exalt the Passover.
To Abraham You were revealed at midnight on Passover.
THIS IS THE PASSOVER FESTIVAL!

דְּלָתָיו דָּפַקְתָּ כְּחֹם הַיּוֹם בַּפֶּסַח. הִסְעִיד נוֹצְצִים עֻגוֹת מַצּוֹת בַּפֶּסַח. וְאֶל־הַבָּקָר רָץ זֵכֶר לְשׁוֹר עֵרֶךְ פֶּסַח.   וַאֲמַרְתֶּם זֶבַח פֶּסַח:

זוֹעֲמוּ סְדוֹמִים וְלוֹהֲטוּ בָאֵשׁ בַּפֶּסַח. חֻלַּץ לוֹט מֵהֶם, וּמַצּוֹת אָפָה בְּקֵץ פֶּסַח. טֵאטֵאתָ אַדְמַת מוֹף וְנוֹף בְּעָבְרְךָ בַּפֶּסַח. וַאֲמַרְתֶּם זֶבַח פֶּסַח:

יָהּ, רֹאשׁ כָּל־אוֹן מָחַצְתָּ בְּלֵיל־שִׁמּוּר פֶּסַח. כַּבִּיר עַל בֵּן בְּכוֹר פָּסַחְתָּ בְּדַם פֶּסַח. לְבִלְתִּי תֵּת מַשְׁחִית לָבֹא בִּפְתָחַי בַּפֶּסַח. וַאֲמַרְתֶּם זֶבַח פֶּסַח:

מְסֻגֶּרֶת סֻגְּרָה בְּעִתּוֹתֵי־פֶּסַח. נִשְׁמְדָה מִדְיָן בִּצְלִיל שְׂעוֹרֵי עֹמֶר פֶּסַח. שֹׂרְפוּ מִשְׁמַנֵּי פּוּל וְלוּד בִּיקַד יְקוֹד פֶּסַח.   וַאֲמַרְתֶּם זֶבַח פֶּסַח:

עוֹד הַיּוֹם בְּנֹב לַעֲמֹד עַד גָּעָה עוֹנַת־פֶּסַח. פַּס יָד כָּתְבָה לְקַעֲקֵעַ צוּל בַּפֶּסַח. צָפֹה הַצָּפִית עָרוֹךְ הַשֻּׁלְחָן בַּפֶּסַח.   וַאֲמַרְתֶּם זֶבַח פֶּסַח:

קָהָל כִּנְּסָה הֲדַסָּה צוֹם לְשַׁלֵּשׁ בַּפֶּסַח. רֹאשׁ מִבֵּית רָשָׁע מָחַצְתָּ בְּעֵץ חֲמִשִּׁים בַּפֶּסַח. שְׁתֵּי אֵלֶּה רֶגַע תָּבִיא לְעוּצִית בַּפֶּסַח. תָּעֹז יָדְךָ וְתָרוּם יְמִינְךָ כְּלֵיל הִתְקַדֶּשׁ חַג פֶּסַח.   וַאֲמַרְתֶּם זֶבַח פֶּסַח:

At the heat of the day You knocked at his doors on Passover.
He prepared for the visitors cakes of unleavened bread on Passover.
And he ran to the herd in anticipation of what we read on Passover.   THIS IS THE PASSOVER FESTIVAL!

The Sodomites provoked God and were consumed by fire on
Passover.
Lot separated from them and baked unleavened bread on Pass-
over.
You swept the land of Egypt when You passed through it on Pass-
over.   THIS IS THE PASSOVER FESTIVAL!

You did smite the first-born on the watchnight of Passover.
You did pass over Israel's first-born on Passover.
You permitted no destroyer to enter Israel's doors on Passover.
        THIS IS THE PASSOVER FESTIVAL!

The walls of Jericho fell on Passover.
Midian was destroyed by a loaf of barley bread measuring
an Omer on Passover.
The soldiers of Pul and Lud were burned in a mighty
conflagration on Passover.
        THIS IS THE PASSOVER FESTIVAL!

Sennacherib met disaster at Zion's gate on Passover.
The hand wrote on the wall in Babylon on Passover.
The table was set and all arranged on Passover.
        THIS IS THE PASSOVER FESTIVAL!

Queen Esther assembled the community to fast three days
at Passover.
Haman was hanged on the gallows fifty cubits high on Passover.
A twofold punishment You will bring on our enemies
on Passover.
Then Your right hand shall be uplifted as on this hallowed
feast of Passover.
        THIS IS THE PASSOVER FESTIVAL!

כִּי לוֹ נָאֶה. כִּי לוֹ יָאֶה:

אַדִּיר בִּמְלוּכָה. בָּחוּר כַּהֲלָכָה. גְּדוּדָיו יֹאמְרוּ לוֹ. לְךָ וּלְךָ. לְךָ כִּי לְךָ. לְךָ
אַף לְךָ. לְךָ יְיָ הַמַּמְלָכָה.

כִּי לוֹ נָאֶה. כִּי לוֹ יָאֶה:

דָּגוּל בִּמְלוּכָה. הָדוּר כַּהֲלָכָה. וָתִיקָיו יֹאמְרוּ לוֹ. לְךָ וּלְךָ. לְךָ כִּי לְךָ. לְךָ
אַף לְךָ. לְךָ יְיָ הַמַּמְלָכָה.

כִּי לוֹ נָאֶה. כִּי לוֹ יָאֶה:

זַכַּאי בִּמְלוּכָה. חָסִין כַּהֲלָכָה. טַפְסְרָיו יֹאמְרוּ לוֹ. לְךָ וּלְךָ. לְךָ כִּי לְךָ. לְךָ
אַף לְךָ. לְךָ יְיָ הַמַּמְלָכָה.

כִּי לוֹ נָאֶה. כִּי לוֹ יָאֶה:

יָחִיד בִּמְלוּכָה. כַּבִּיר כַּהֲלָכָה. לִמּוּדָיו יֹאמְרוּ לוֹ. לְךָ וּלְךָ. לְךָ כִּי לְךָ. לְךָ
אַף לְךָ. לְךָ יְיָ הַמַּמְלָכָה.

כִּי לוֹ נָאֶה. כִּי לוֹ יָאֶה:

מוֹשֵׁל בִּמְלוּכָה. נוֹרָא כַּהֲלָכָה. סְבִיבָיו יֹאמְרוּ לוֹ. לְךָ וּלְךָ. לְךָ כִּי לְךָ.
לְךָ אַף לְךָ. לְךָ יְיָ הַמַּמְלָכָה.

כִּי לוֹ נָאֶה. כִּי לוֹ יָאֶה:

עָנָו בִּמְלוּכָה. פּוֹדֶה כַּהֲלָכָה. צַדִּיקָיו יֹאמְרוּ לוֹ. לְךָ וּלְךָ. לְךָ כִּי לְךָ. לְךָ
אַף לְךָ. לְךָ יְיָ הַמַּמְלָכָה.

כִּי לוֹ נָאֶה. כִּי לוֹ יָאֶה:

קָדוֹשׁ בִּמְלוּכָה. רַחוּם כַּהֲלָכָה. שִׁנְאַנָּיו יֹאמְרוּ לוֹ. לְךָ וּלְךָ. לְךָ כִּי לְךָ.
לְךָ אַף לְךָ. לְךָ יְיָ הַמַּמְלָכָה.

כִּי לוֹ נָאֶה. כִּי לוֹ יָאֶה:

תַּקִּיף בִּמְלוּכָה. תּוֹמֵךְ כַּהֲלָכָה. תְּמִימָיו יֹאמְרוּ לוֹ. לְךָ וּלְךָ. לְךָ כִּי לְךָ.
לְךָ אַף לְךָ. לְךָ יְיָ הַמַּמְלָכָה.

כִּי לוֹ נָאֶה. כִּי לוֹ יָאֶה:

TO HIM IT IS FITTING, TO HIM IT IS DUE.

Mighty in majesty, Supreme indeed! His legions sing to Him:
Yours alone, O God, is the world's sovereignty.
TO HIM IT IS FITTING, TO HIM IT IS DUE.

First in majesty, Glorious indeed! His faithful sing to Him:
Yours alone, O God, is the world's sovereignty.
TO HIM IT IS FITTING, TO HIM IT IS DUE.

Pure in majesty, Powerful indeed! His attendants sing to Him:
Yours alone, O God, is the world's sovereignty.
TO HIM IT IS FITTING, TO HIM IT IS DUE.

Unique in majesty, Mighty indeed! His disciples sing to Him:
Yours alone, O God, is the world's sovereignty.
TO HIM IT IS FITTING, TO HIM IT IS DUE.

Ruling in majesty, Revered indeed! His angels sing to Him:
Yours alone, O God, is the world's sovereignty.
TO HIM IT IS FITTING, TO HIM IT IS DUE.

Humble in majesty, Redeemer indeed! His righteous sing to Him:
Yours alone, O God, is the world's sovereignty.
TO HIM IT IS FITTING, TO HIM IT IS DUE.

Holy in majesty, Merciful indeed! His myriads sing to Him:
Yours alone, O God, is the world's sovereignty.
TO HIM IT IS FITTING, TO HIM IT IS DUE.

Almighty in majesty, Sustainer indeed! His upright sing to Him:
Yours alone, O God, is the world's sovereignty.
TO HIM IT IS FITTING, TO HIM IT IS DUE.

אַדִּיר הוּא

אַדִּיר הוּא.

יִבְנֶה בֵיתוֹ בְּקָרוֹב. בִּמְהֵרָה בִּמְהֵרָה, בְּיָמֵינוּ בְּקָרוֹב. אֵל בְּנֵה. אֵל בְּנֵה.
בְּנֵה בֵיתְךָ בְּקָרוֹב:

בָּחוּר הוּא. גָּדוֹל הוּא. דָּגוּל הוּא.

יִבְנֶה בֵיתוֹ בְּקָרוֹב. בִּמְהֵרָה בִּמְהֵרָה, בְּיָמֵינוּ בְּקָרוֹב. אֵל בְּנֵה. אֵל בְּנֵה.
בְּנֵה בֵיתְךָ בְּקָרוֹב:

הָדוּר הוּא. וָתִיק הוּא. זַכַּאי הוּא. חָסִיד הוּא.

יִבְנֶה בֵיתוֹ בְּקָרוֹב. בִּמְהֵרָה בִּמְהֵרָה, בְּיָמֵינוּ בְּקָרוֹב. אֵל בְּנֵה. אֵל בְּנֵה.
בְּנֵה בֵיתְךָ בְּקָרוֹב:

טָהוֹר הוּא. יָחִיד הוּא. כַּבִּיר הוּא.

לָמוּד הוּא. מֶלֶךְ הוּא. נוֹרָא הוּא.

סַגִּיב הוּא. עִזּוּז הוּא. פּוֹדֶה הוּא. צַדִּיק הוּא.

יִבְנֶה בֵיתוֹ בְּקָרוֹב. בִּמְהֵרָה בִּמְהֵרָה, בְּיָמֵינוּ בְּקָרוֹב. אֵל בְּנֵה. אֵל בְּנֵה.
בְּנֵה בֵיתְךָ בְּקָרוֹב.

קָדוֹשׁ הוּא. רַחוּם הוּא. שַׁדַּי הוּא. תַּקִּיף הוּא.

יִבְנֶה בֵיתוֹ בְּקָרוֹב. בִּמְהֵרָה בִּמְהֵרָה, בְּיָמֵינוּ בְּקָרוֹב. אֵל בְּנֵה. אֵל בְּנֵה.
בְּנֵה בֵיתְךָ בְּקָרוֹב:

ADIR HU

God is Mighty!
  May He soon rebuild His Temple.
Speedily, speedily,
  In our days, soon.
O God, rebuild, O God, rebuild,
  Rebuild Your Temple soon.

God is First, Great and Renowned!
  May He soon rebuild His Temple.
Speedily, speedily,
  In our days, soon.
O God, rebuild, O God, rebuild,
  Rebuild Your Temple soon.

He is Glorious, Faithful, Just and Gracious!
  May He soon rebuild His Temple.
Speedily, speedily,
  In our days, soon.
O God, rebuild, O God, rebuild,
  Rebuild Your Temple soon.

He is Pure, Unique, Mighty, Wise, Majestic,
Revered, Exalted, Strong, Redeemer and Righteous!
  May He soon rebuild His Temple.
Speedily, speedily,
  In our days, soon.
O God, rebuild, O God, rebuild,
  Rebuild Your Temple soon.

He is Holy, Merciful Powerful, Almighty!
  May He soon rebuild His Temple.
Speedily, speedily,
  In our days, soon.
O God, rebuild, O God, rebuild,
  Rebuild Your Temple soon.

אֶחָד מִי יוֹדֵעַ?

אֶחָד מִי יוֹדֵעַ? אֶחָד אֲנִי יוֹדֵעַ. אֶחָד אֱלֹהֵינוּ שֶׁבַּשָּׁמַיִם וּבָאָרֶץ:

שְׁנַיִם מִי יוֹדֵעַ? שְׁנַיִם אֲנִי יוֹדֵעַ. שְׁנֵי לֻחוֹת־הַבְּרִית. אֶחָד אֱלֹהֵינוּ שֶׁבַּשָּׁמַיִם וּבָאָרֶץ:

שְׁלֹשָׁה מִי יוֹדֵעַ? שְׁלֹשָׁה אֲנִי יוֹדֵעַ. שְׁלֹשָׁה אָבוֹת. שְׁנֵי לֻחוֹת־הַבְּרִית. אֶחָד אֱלֹהֵינוּ שֶׁבַּשָּׁמַיִם וּבָאָרֶץ:

אַרְבַּע מִי יוֹדֵעַ? אַרְבַּע אֲנִי יוֹדֵעַ. אַרְבַּע אִמָּהוֹת. שְׁלֹשָׁה אָבוֹת. שְׁנֵי־לֻחוֹת הַבְּרִית. אֶחָד אֱלֹהֵינוּ שֶׁבַּשָּׁמַיִם וּבָאָרֶץ:

חֲמִשָּׁה מִי יוֹדֵעַ? חֲמִשָּׁה אֲנִי יוֹדֵעַ. חֲמִשָּׁה חוּמְשֵׁי־תוֹרָה. אַרְבַּע אִמָּהוֹת. שְׁלֹשָׁה אָבוֹת. שְׁנֵי לֻחוֹת־הַבְּרִית. אֶחָד אֱלֹהֵינוּ שֶׁבַּשָּׁמַיִם וּבָאָרֶץ:

שִׁשָּׁה מִי יוֹדֵעַ? שִׁשָּׁה אֲנִי יוֹדֵעַ. שִׁשָּׁה סִדְרֵי־מִשְׁנָה. חֲמִשָּׁה חוּמְשֵׁי־תוֹרָה. אַרְבַּע אִמָּהוֹת. שְׁלֹשָׁה אָבוֹת. שְׁנֵי לֻחוֹת־הַבְּרִית. אֶחָד אֱלֹהֵינוּ שֶׁבַּשָּׁמַיִם וּבָאָרֶץ:

EḤAD MI YODE'A?

Who knows one? I know one.
One is our God, in heaven and on earth.

Who knows two? I know two.
Two are the tablets of the covenant;
One is our God, in heaven and on earth.

Who knows three? I know three.
Three are the patriarchs;
Two are the tablets of the covenant;
One is our God, in heaven and on earth.

Who knows four? I know four.
Four are the matriarchs;
Three are the patriarchs;
Two are the tablets of the covenant;
One is our God, in heaven and on earth.

Who knows five? I know five.
Five are the books of the Torah;
Four are the matriarchs;
Three are the patriarchs;
Two are the tablets of the covenant;
One is our God, in heaven and on earth.

Who knows six? I know six.
Six are the sections of the Mishnah;
Five are the books of the Torah;
Four are the matriarchs;
Three are the patriarchs;
Two are the tablets of the covenant;
One is our God, in heaven and on earth.

שִׁבְעָה מִי יוֹדֵעַ? שִׁבְעָה אֲנִי יוֹדֵעַ. שִׁבְעָה יְמֵי־שַׁבַּתָּא. שִׁשָּׁה סִדְרֵי־ מִשְׁנָה. חֲמִשָּׁה חוּמְשֵׁי־תוֹרָה. אַרְבַּע אִמָּהוֹת. שְׁלשָׁה אָבוֹת. שְׁנֵי לֻחוֹת־הַבְּרִית. אֶחָד אֱלֹהֵינוּ שֶׁבַּשָּׁמַיִם וּבָאָרֶץ:

שְׁמוֹנָה מִי יוֹדֵעַ? שְׁמוֹנָה אֲנִי יוֹדֵעַ. שְׁמוֹנָה יְמֵי־מִילָה. שִׁבְעָה יְמֵי־ שַׁבַּתָּא. שִׁשָּׁה סִדְרֵי־מִשְׁנָה. חֲמִשָּׁה חוּמְשֵׁי־תוֹרָה. אַרְבַּע אִמָּהוֹת. שְׁלשָׁה אָבוֹת. שְׁנֵי לֻחוֹת־הַבְּרִית. אֶחָד אֱלֹהֵינוּ שֶׁבַּשָּׁמַיִם וּבָאָרֶץ:

תִּשְׁעָה מִי יוֹדֵעַ? תִּשְׁעָה אֲנִי יוֹדֵעַ. תִּשְׁעָה יַרְחֵי־לֵדָה. שְׁמוֹנָה יְמֵי־ מִילָה. שִׁבְעָה יְמֵי־שַׁבַּתָּא. שִׁשָּׁה סִדְרֵי־מִשְׁנָה. חֲמִשָּׁה חוּמְשֵׁי־תוֹרָה. אַרְבַּע אִמָּהוֹת. שְׁלשָׁה אָבוֹת. שְׁנֵי לֻחוֹת־הַבְּרִית. אֶחָד אֱלֹהֵינוּ שֶׁבַּשָּׁמַיִם וּבָאָרֶץ:

עֲשָׂרָה מִי יוֹדֵעַ? עֲשָׂרָה אֲנִי יוֹדֵעַ. עֲשָׂרָה דִּבְּרַיָּא. תִּשְׁעָה יַרְחֵי־לֵדָה. שְׁמוֹנָה יְמֵי־מִילָה. שִׁבְעָה יְמֵי־שַׁבַּתָּא. שִׁשָּׁה סִדְרֵי־מִשְׁנָה. חֲמִשָּׁה חוּמְשֵׁי־תוֹרָה. אַרְבַּע אִמָּהוֹת. שְׁלשָׁה אָבוֹת. שְׁנֵי לֻחוֹת־הַבְּרִית. אֶחָד אֱלֹהֵינוּ שֶׁבַּשָּׁמַיִם וּבָאָרֶץ:

Who knows seven? I know seven.
Seven are the days of the week;
Six are the sections of the Mishnah;
Five are the books of the Torah;
Four are the matriarchs;
Three are the patriarchs;
Two are the tablets of the covenant;
One is our God, in heaven and on earth.

Who knows eight? I know eight.
Eight are the days of circumcision;
Seven are the days of the week;
Six are the sections of the Mishnah;
Five are the books of the Torah;
Four are the matriarchs;
Three are the patriarchs;
Two are the tablets of the covenant;
One is our God, in heaven and on earth.

Who knows nine? I know nine.
Nine are the months of childbirth;
Eight are the days of circumcision;
Seven are the days of the week;
Six are the sections of the Mishnah;
Five are the books of the Torah;
Four are the matriarchs;
Three are the patriarchs;
Two are the tablets of the covenant;
One is our God, in heaven and on earth.

Who knows ten? I know ten.
Ten are the commandments;
Nine are the months of childbirth;
Eight are the days of circumcision;
Seven are the days of the week;
Six are the sections of the Mishnah;

אֶחָד עָשָׂר מִי יוֹדֵעַ? אֶחָד עָשָׂר אֲנִי יוֹדֵעַ. אַחַד עָשָׂר כּוֹכְבַיָּא. עֲשָׂרָה
דִּבְּרַיָּא. תִּשְׁעָה יַרְחֵי־לֵדָה. שְׁמוֹנָה יְמֵי־מִילָה. שִׁבְעָה יְמֵי־שַׁבַּתָּא.
שִׁשָּׁה סִדְרֵי־מִשְׁנָה. חֲמִשָּׁה חוּמְשֵׁי־תוֹרָה. אַרְבַּע אִמָּהוֹת. שְׁלֹשָׁה
אָבוֹת. שְׁנֵי לֻחוֹת־הַבְּרִית. אֶחָד אֱלֹהֵינוּ שֶׁבַּשָּׁמַיִם וּבָאָרֶץ:

שְׁנֵים עָשָׂר מִי יוֹדֵעַ? שְׁנֵים עָשָׂר אֲנִי יוֹדֵעַ. שְׁנֵים עָשָׂר שִׁבְטַיָּא. אַחַד
עָשָׂר כּוֹכְבַיָּא. עֲשָׂרָה דִּבְּרַיָּא. תִּשְׁעָה יַרְחֵי־לֵדָה. שְׁמוֹנָה יְמֵי־מִילָה.
שִׁבְעָה יְמֵי־שַׁבַּתָּא. שִׁשָּׁה סִדְרֵי־מִשְׁנָה. חֲמִשָּׁה חוּמְשֵׁי־תוֹרָה. אַרְבַּע
אִמָּהוֹת. שְׁלֹשָׁה אָבוֹת. שְׁנֵי לֻחוֹת־הַבְּרִית. אֶחָד אֱלֹהֵינוּ שֶׁבַּשָּׁמַיִם
וּבָאָרֶץ:

שְׁלֹשָׁה עָשָׂר מִי יוֹדֵעַ? שְׁלֹשָׁה עָשָׂר אֲנִי יוֹדֵעַ. שְׁלֹשָׁה עָשָׂר מִדַּיָּא.
שְׁנֵים עָשָׂר שִׁבְטַיָּא. אַחַד עָשָׂר כּוֹכְבַיָּא. עֲשָׂרָה דִּבְּרַיָּא. תִּשְׁעָה יַרְחֵי־

Five are the books of the Torah;
Four are the matriarchs;
Three are the patriarchs;
Two are the tablets of the covenant;
One is our God, in heaven and on earth.

Who knows eleven? I know eleven.
Eleven are the stars in Joseph's dream;
Ten are the commandments;
Nine are the months of childbirth;
Eight are the days of circumcision;
Seven are the days of the week;
Six are the sections of the Mishnah;
Five are the books of the Torah;
Four are the matriarchs;
Three are the patriarchs;
Two are the tablets of the covenant;
One is our God, in heaven and on earth.

Who knows twelve? I know twelve.
Twelve are the tribes of Israel;
Eleven are the stars in Joseph's dream;
Ten are the commandments;
Nine are the months of childbirth;
Eight are the days of circumcision;
Seven are the days of the week;
Six are the sections of the Mishnah;
Five are the books of the Torah;
Four are the matriarchs;
Three are the patriarchs;
Two are the tablets of the Covenant;
One is our God, in heaven and on earth.

Who knows thirteen? I know thirteen.
Thirteen are God's attributes;
Twelve, the tribes, of Israel;
Eleven, the stars in Joseph's dream;

לֵדָה. שְׁמוֹנָה יְמֵי־מִילָה. שִׁבְעָה יְמֵי־שַׁבַּתָּא. שִׁשָּׁה סִדְרֵי־מִשְׁנָה.
חֲמִשָּׁה חוּמְשֵׁי־תוֹרָה. אַרְבַּע אִמָּהוֹת. שְׁלֹשָׁה אָבוֹת. שְׁנֵי לֻחוֹת־
הַבְּרִית. אֶחָד אֱלֹהֵינוּ שֶׁבַּשָּׁמַיִם וּבָאָרֶץ:

חַד גַּדְיָא

חַד גַּדְיָא. חַד גַּדְיָא. דְּזַבַּן אַבָּא בִּתְרֵי זוּזֵי. חַד גַּדְיָא. חַד גַּדְיָא:

וְאָתָא שׁוּנְרָא. וְאָכְלָה לְגַּדְיָא. דְּזַבַּן אַבָּא בִּתְרֵי זוּזֵי. חַד גַּדְיָא. חַד
גַּדְיָא:

וְאָתָא כַלְבָּא. וְנָשַׁךְ לְשׁוּנְרָא. דְּאָכְלָה לְגַּדְיָא. דְּזַבַּן אַבָּא בִּתְרֵי זוּזֵי. חַד
גַּדְיָא. חַד גַּדְיָא:

וְאָתָא חוּטְרָא. וְהִכָּה לְכַלְבָּא דְּנָשַׁךְ לְשׁוּנְרָא. דְּאָכְלָה לְגַּדְיָא. דְּזַבַּן אַבָּא
בִּתְרֵי זוּזֵי. חַד גַּדְיָא:

וְאָתָא נוּרָא. וְשָׂרַף לְחוּטְרָא. דְּהִכָּה לְכַלְבָּא דְּנָשַׁךְ לְשׁוּנְרָא. דְּאָכְלָה
לְגַּדְיָא. דְּזַבַּן אַבָּא בִּתְרֵי זוּזֵי. חַד גַּדְיָא. חַד גַּדְיָא:

Ten are the commandments;
Nine are the months of childbirth;
Eight are the days of circumcision;
Seven are the days of the week;
Six are the sections of the Mishnah;
Five are the books of the Torah;
Four are the matriarchs;
Three are the patriarchs;
Two are the tablets of the covenant;
One is our God, in heaven and on earth.

ḤAD GADYA

One little goat, one little goat,
  My father bought for two zuzim.
One little goat, one little goat.

Then came a cat and ate the goat
  My father bought for two zuzim.
One little goat, one little goat.

Then came a dog and bit the cat,
  That ate the goat
My father bought for two zuzim.
  One little goat, one little goat.

Then came a stick and beat the dog,
  That bit the cat that ate the goat
My father bought for two zuzim.
  One little goat, one little goat.

Then came a fire and burned the stick,
  That beat the dog that bit the cat
That ate the goat
  My father bought for two zuzim.
One little goat, one little goat.

וְאָתָא מַיָּא. וְכָבָה לְנוּרָא. דְּשָׂרַף לְחוּטְרָא. דְּהִכָּה לְכַלְבָּא. דְּנָשַׁךְ לְשׁוּנְרָא. דְּאָכְלָה לְגַדְיָא. דְּזַבֵּן אַבָּא בִּתְרֵי זוּזֵי. חַד גַּדְיָא. חַד גַּדְיָא:

וְאָתָא תוֹרָא. וְשָׁתָה לְמַיָּא. דְּכָבָה לְנוּרָא. דְּשָׂרַף לְחוּטְרָא. דְּהִכָּה לְכַלְבָּא. דְּנָשַׁךְ לְשׁוּנְרָא. דְּאָכְלָה לְגַדְיָא. דְּזַבֵּן אַבָּא בִּתְרֵי זוּזֵי. חַד גַּדְיָא. חַד גַּדְיָא:

וְאָתָא הַשּׁוֹחֵט. וְשָׁחַט לְתוֹרָא. דְּשָׁתָה לְמַיָּא. דְּכָבָה לְנוּרָא. דְּשָׂרַף לְחוּטְרָא. דְּהִכָּה לְכַלְבָּא. דְּנָשַׁךְ לְשׁוּנְרָא. דְּאָכְלָה לְגַדְיָא. דְּזַבֵּן אַבָּא בִּתְרֵי זוּזֵי. חַד גַּדְיָא. חַד גַּדְיָא:

וְאָתָא מַלְאַךְ הַמָּוֶת. וְשָׁחַט לְשׁוֹחֵט דְּשָׁחַט לְתוֹרָא. דְּשָׁתָה לְמַיָּא. דְּכָבָה לְנוּרָא. דְּשָׂרַף לְחוּטְרָא. דְּהִכָּה לְכַלְבָּא. דְּנָשַׁךְ לְשׁוּנְרָא. דְּאָכְלָה לְגַדְיָא. דְּזַבֵּן אַבָּא בִּתְרֵי זוּזֵי. חַד גַּדְיָא. חַד גַּדְיָא:

וְאָתָא הַקָּדוֹשׁ בָּרוּךְ הוּא. וְשָׁחַט לְמַלְאַךְ הַמָּוֶת. דְּשָׁחַט לְשׁוֹחֵט. דְּשָׁחַט לְתוֹרָא. דְּשָׁתָה לְמַיָּא. דְּכָבָה לְנוּרָא, דְּשָׂרַף לְחוּטְרָא. דְּהִכָּה לְכַלְבָּא. דְּנָשַׁךְ לְשׁוּנְרָא. דְּאָכְלָה לְגַדְיָא. דְּזַבֵּן אַבָּא בִּתְרֵי זוּזֵי. חַד גַּדְיָא. חַד גַּדְיָא:

Then came the water and quenched the fire,
  That burned the stick that beat the dog
That bit the cat that ate the goat
  My father bought for two zuzim.
One little goat, one little goat.

Then came an ox and drank the water,
  That quenched the fire that burned the stick
That beat the dog that bit the cat
  That ate the goat
My father bought for two zuzim
  One little goat, one little goat.

Then came a *shoḥet* and slaughtered the ox,
  That drank the water that quenched the fire
That burned the stick that beat the dog
  That bit the cat that ate the goat
My father bought for two zuzim
  One little goat, one little goat.

Then came the angel of death and killed the *shoḥet*,
  That slaughtered the ox that drank the water
That quenched the fire that burned the stick
  That beat the dog that bit the cat
That ate the goat
  My father bought for two zuzim.
One little goat, one little goat.

Then came the Holy One, blessed be He,
  And slew the angel of death,
That killed the *shoḥet* that slaughtered the ox
  That drank the water that quenched the fire
That burned the stick that beat the dog
  That bit the cat that ate the goat
My father bought for two zuzim.
  One little goat, one little goat.